30 DAILY DEVOTIONALS & DISCUSSION GUIDES

The Gift

UNWRAPPING GOD'S DESIGN
FOR FOSTER CARE & ADOPTION

PAM PARISH

FOREWORD BY: JEDD MEDEFIND

The Gift

Unwrapping God's Design for Foster Care & Adoption

Put your trust in the Lord. Walk steadily along His path." (Psalm 27:34)
Like a trusted friend who has walked courageously through both the
beautiful and difficult journeys in life, Pam Parish shares biblical truth about
adoption and foster care in a devotional that dives deep and yet allows
space for personal reflection and Spirit-led response. She carefully tends to
each scripture in James 1, offering thought-provoking insight and battle-
tested wisdom. The Gift is just that – a thoughtful and practical gift for
those considering foster care and adoption, and for those who want to
serve orphans and vulnerable children well.

Ronne Rock, *Orphan Outreach*

Pam takes us on a journey to see how our story [and hers] can be found in
the words of the Apostle Paul in James 1. Through this devotional our eyes
are opened to the privilege we have as foster and adoptive parents to 'count
it all joy' and embrace the heart of God for us.

Whitney Bunker, *A City Without Orphans*

Pam has done it again. She's created an in-depth study for those of us who
welcome children from hard places into our homes. This devotional delves
deeply into our personal walk with Jesus, challenging us to honestly assess
our motives and our actions, according to biblical truth. Each devotion
ends with penetrating and introspective questions that truly help us grow
and change together.

Johnna Stein, *Promise 686*

Reading through *The Gift* as an early reader for Pam meant I would need to move quickly and skip reflection, journaling, and the greater joy of spending time praying over each devotion and question. Yet I found myself stopping mid-stream and thinking about how the experiences of our adoption and foster care journey still bring strong emotions. We never forget how we failed at times and felt like a "bad parent." I recalled how my beautiful adoptive daughter one time, in anger, said to me, "Why did you adopt me, I could have had a good mom."

Pam so beautifully reminds us that although we aren't, or weren't, the perfect parent, we are loved by our Heavenly Father and He will never turn His back on us. What a gift to have been able to walk through the adoption journey and to be able to look back and see the fruit of the years. *The Gift* again and again affirms the challenges, and more importantly the reasons and pearls, for checking our armor daily and going forward with determination—even when we are battle-weary. Every foster and adoptive parent needs to carry *The Gift* close to them. When you feeling beaten, confused or just plain out of sorts—stop and read—reflect, write, pray, and then recognized how blessed you are for such gifts in your own life.

Ruby Johnston, *LAMb International*

The Gift is rich in His truth and with each devotional—I found myself being more still to take in each word, each scripture reference, each prayer and story as together they all drew me closer to the Giver Himself. This book was more than just a devotional to me—but an invitation to remember who He is and who I am in Him—and an opportunity to simply sit at His table. It's here that all my needs are met—and it's also here where He fills me to go and be who He has called me to be. This devotional will take you deeper to His heart if you do it alone, but just like Pam says—together is even better. After taking it in by myself I can't wait to share it with my spouse and hear his reflections. This would also be a wonderful devotional to use in a Bible study or even a small group if you are wanting to go deeper to His heart together! As a mom of 6 children (both biological and adopted) juggling much as we embark on another decade on the board with Wiphan, an orphan/widow ministry in Zambia, its so important for us to experience His healing, power and rest so we may lead others into the same gifts from Him. I can't wait to have our teachers and staff read and rest in these truths in *The Gift*. May we walk into His ways with freedom, joy and strength! With Christ—truly the best is yet to come! Thank you Pam for reminding me and pointing my eyes UP!

Andrea Young, *Created for Care*

Real transparency and authentic love is the recurring theme in *The Gift*. Pam's inviting writing style makes you feel as if you are sitting together around the table over a cup of coffee and sharing life. We bear silent witness to her tremendous testimony of following her God-given calling, loving well and relentlessly fighting for those experiencing isolation and desperately in need of family. The words of encouragement she offers straight from The Father's heart instills such hope to all who are living out their calling in the foster and adoption community and more. The honesty she reveals in the difficult days and seasons as you love and serve are refreshing and inspiring to others in the trenches of redemption or on the celebratory mountaintops. Grateful for friends like Pam who continuously pour into others along the way. Finding friends and wrap around support from those who "get it" is vital. Pam is one of those friends we are all blessed to know and love.

Mandy Litzke, *Safe Harbor Orphan Care Ministries*

The Gift

Unwrapping God's Design

for Foster Care & Adoption

30 Daily Devotions & Discussion Guides

Written By:

Pam Parish

Foreword By:

Jedd Medefind

Editors: Johnna Stein & Kristan Bhandari
Cover Art: Big Stock Photography
Cover Design: German Creative
Author Photo: Craig Obrist Photography
Inspiration: Every foster and adoptive family that I've ever met.

ISBN: 996492801
ISBN-13: 978-0-9964928-0-5

DEDICATION

This book is dedicated to my loved ones who have passed on from this life and entered into their eternal rest in the past two years of my life. Especially to my Daddy & Momma, Leonard Wayne Gary & Lena Yvonne Marcus, I miss you both dearly. And to my friend Mallory whose influence on my life touches every page of this book, I know you're hosting sparkle parties in heaven and I can't wait to join you one day. Until then, I will choose to see the joy in every day and worship Jesus with abandon regardless of my circumstances, in these things you were my greatest teacher.

And to...

"Momma" Pam Minton, Terry Watts, Pastor Sam Mayo, Jennifer Poe, Mamaw Faye Gary, Mamaw Mary Parish, Uncle Terry Gary, Uncle Dennis Long and my precious black lab, Chester. Your fingerprints (and paw prints) on my life will never be forgotten. Until I see you again, I love you.

To those reading this page, take a moment and text a few people who mean the world to you. Tomorrow isn't promised and you will miss them far more than you know when they are absent from your life. Choose to see the value of every person that God has given you to love.

CONTENTS

ACKNOWLEDGMENTS

The Gift has been my constant companion for more than three years. I've been teaching James Chapter One whenever I speak or lead a workshop for all this time. Many times after a session someone would ask, "Is this in a devotional somewhere?" And my answer was always, "Not yet. God hasn't released me to write it yet." In hindsight the truth wasn't that He hadn't released me to write it, He simply wasn't finished with it *in* me yet. Living out the truth of these scriptures through the crucible of the last few years has taught me just how utterly faithful Jesus is to me. I want to always acknowledge Him first in everything that I do because, without Him, I honestly think my soul would have been crushed. Second only to Jesus is my wonderful husband, or as I prefer to call him—my boyfriend of more than 27 years and counting, Steve. You've held me many times over the past few years as my heart broke in grief and loss. You've covered me in prayer and encouraged me when I didn't think I could find the energy to get up and face another day. You are my rock and my very best friend. To say I'm thankful for you is a vast understatement, you are my everything.

To our daughters, grand-children and sons-in-law—Candie, Katya, Tae & Kelsey, Tyree & Seara, Elizabeth, Charlie, Paul & Kristan, Heather, Juan, Jayden, Adrianna, and Junior—I love you so much. You make my life full and I'm honored that you call me mom and Nana. You are God's greatest gifts to me. I've been honored by you as you've dropped everything in your own adult lives to drive six hours to Kentucky, on multiple occasions, and stand beside me as we said our final goodbyes to dear family members. I've watched you each bravely face all the struggles of "adulting" and learn to "count it all joy" even in the midst of the hard and hurtful parts of life. As a family we've walked through grief, we've celebrated new love, and we've grown to value and trust one another in ways that only the passing of time and shared experience can produce. I wouldn't want to do this thing called life with any other crazy family. You guys are my world.

Both of my prior books have included a paragraph "To our parents…" in the acknowledgements. This is the first title I've written without my parents on this earth and without my Dad chomping at the bit waiting on his first copy. I miss them and learning to live without them on this earth will be a lifelong process. Even so, I'm so grateful for those people that God has placed in my life who love and cover me as parents and family. To my wonderful, amazing, incredible, phenomenal, and any other terrific adjective you can come up with, mother and father-in-law, Gary & Janice Parish. You two are a treasure beyond words. I'm so grateful to be a Parish and to have been given the privilege of being a part of your family on earth. To my Aunt Connie Gary, there's no one that I would have rather had beside me as Daddy transitioned from earth to heaven. Your constant reassuring presence and expertise were a grounding force for me. Thank you isn't enough. I love you so much. To my Uncle Garland & Aunt Patsy Brown, Uncle Jerry & Aunt Brenda, Uncle Ray & Aunt Martha Brown, my brother Steve Gary, my sister-in-law Wendy Gary, my sister and brother-in-law Hondo & Becky Clayton, Papaw James Parish, Rodger & Anna Beth Parish, my "sister" and her husband Chad & Tandi Howard, Jeremy & Emily Hopwood (and Grace, Cole, Ella & Ethan), George & Debbie Stull, Zack & Carrington Crowe (and Aurora), Chaz & Kayla (and Drake), and my nieces and nephews—Joshua & Crystal Tanner, Austin Ferguson, Brandon Gary, Shelby Gary, Patrick Gullett & Seth Gullet, I love all of you and am so very thankful to have you in my life. Your influence is evident throughout the pages of this book.

To everyone who participated in this book coming to pass, thank you. To Jedd Medefind, your Foreword still brings me to tears. It's beautiful. I'm thankful for your friendship and consider it an honor to watch your leadership for the orphan care movement worldwide. To Johnna Stein, my friend and editor. Your patience for my misuse of the oxford comma and love of "threes" is a blessing. Thank you for your encouragement and feedback through the editing process. To Kristan Bhandari, my daughter and editor. Thank you for your candid feedback, humorous editing notes and forgiveness of my abusive semi-colon usage. It blesses me that you enjoy reading your mom's musings and always have such encouraging things to say.

Many people count themselves lucky to participate in one good church, I'm grateful to be a part of two church families—Victory World Church (Norcross, GA) & Journey Church (Loganville, GA). To my pastors Dennis & Colleen Rouse and Ken & Julie Sirmens, I'm grateful for your leadership, encouragement, and wholehearted devotion to God and His Word. My life and the life of our entire family is shaped by you.

To some of the most important people in my life, my friends and mentors: "G'ma" Harriette Crain, Glen & Taylor Scott, Chrissy Strohmeyer, Larry Combs, Gabrielle Jewel, Amanda Jewel, Kyle & Allison Cruz (and Lilian), Kyle & Jess Purintun, Danielle Cruz, Charlie & Erin Pike, Nathan & Ashley Williams, Montell & Kristin Jordan, Chris & Catharine Jordan, Kurt Scobie & Elizabeth Blakemore, Jeff & Ashley Charron, Gary & Paula Walderich, Jerry & Martha Rick, Andy & Sandra Stanley, Kevin & Lesli Reece, Julia Amendola, Andre & Ronetta Slaughter, Ronne Rock, Mindy Park, Phil & Mary Jane Wolfe, Reid & Hope Hailey, Barry & Tricia White, Russell & Lisa Qualls, Melody Frcek, Laura Engelbrecht, Sid & Jacquie Bohannan,

Lindsay Reeves, John & Deena Thiess, Ryan & Crystal Casey, Chad & Beth Whiteside, Lareasa Mettler, Joe & Cindy Gabard, Merideth Douglas, Bennie Cruz, Andrea Young, Daniel & Whitney Bunker, Lynn & Ruby Johnston, Ernie & Cheryl Johnson, David & Jane Schooler, Jason & Dawn Wright, Amy Wilkinson Curtis, Toni Steere, Lisa Ferris Johnson, Jason Weber, Jason Johnson, Elizabeth Wiebe, Andy Cook, Ty & Kristen Bryant, Amy Holman, Ashley Phelan, Denise Cox, David & Lisa Hennessey, Tony & Katie Gonzalez, Amy Huston Callahan, Carol Kochon, Charles & Kristin Santa Maria, Daniel & Julie Homrich, Gregg & Josie Pawlowski, Ryan & Christi Howard, Willie & Kori Robertson, John & Chrys Howard, Wayne & Kelli Naugle, Rodger Naugle, Maridel Sandberg, Andrew & Michele Schniedler, Beth Templeton, Karen Springs, David & Amber Stephens, Mandy Litzke, Johnson & Summer Bowie, Michael & Carrie Buckingham, Ty & Rebecca Buckingham, Elijah & Stephanie Tindall, Samela Macon, Jeff Jones, Susan Williams, and Teddy & Debbie Kavadas. God has unquestionably blessed me beyond measure in the area of friendships. I am eternally grateful for each of you.

It is the privilege of my life that God has granted me the honor of launching an organization like Connections Homes which takes part of our family's story and makes it reality for other families who desire to step into the story of a young adult who has no one else. To the team of people who surround me in this vision, I can't thank you enough. You take my small ideas and make them big. David & Jeni Nitzel, Shane & Amy Fatzinger, Laura McTier, Sheena Ducat, Erika Johnson, Toni Freeman, Andrie Baker, and Brittany Richards. From me and the 62 young adults whose lives have been forever changed because of you—THANK YOU.

So, MY VERY DEAR FRIENDS, DON'T GET THROWN OFF COURSE. EVERY DESIRABLE AND BENEFICIAL GIFT COMES OUT OF HEAVEN. THE GIFTS ARE RIVERS OF LIGHT CASCADING DOWN FROM THE FATHER OF LIGHT. THERE IS NOTHING DECEITFUL IN GOD, NOTHING TWO-FACED, NOTHING FICKLE. HE BROUGHT US TO LIFE USING THE TRUE WORD, SHOWING US OFF AS THE CROWN OF ALL HIS CREATURES.

JAMES 1:16-18 (MSG)

INTRODUCTION

As I set out to write this book the first signs of fall are starting—leaves are falling and turning beautiful shades of color, days are warm and evenings are cool, and Starbucks has brought back Pumpkin Spice seasonal drinks, a good and perfect gift indeed. The hot, humid days of another "Hotlanta" summer are drawing to a close and, for me, the sounds of jingle bells are beginning to chime. If it wouldn't require me to update this copy every single day, I would tell you how exactly how many days, minutes and seconds are left until Christmas. Trust me, I know.

I love Christmas. The call for Christmas lists goes out in July to all of my kids because it gives me great pleasure to shop for things that make them happy. I start months in advance in anticipation of watching them open gifts that I've thoughtfully purchased, beautifully wrapped and uniquely tagged specifically for each child and grandchild. Many of the gifts that are opened that day have sat hidden away for months until the day came to wrap them and set them under the tree, displayed proudly as a token of our great love toward our family.

The gifts are not broken, they are not used, they are not something that is unwanted. Each gift is unique and lovingly selected with a specific loved one in mind; gifts meant to bring pleasure or meet a need. There are no trick gifts, there are no junk gifts, there are no gifts meant to shame, there are no gifts meant to harm and there are no greater gifts given to one child over another. The gifts are different, equal and uniquely meant to bless; even if one gift is a pair of shoes and another is an electronic device. Each gift is chosen and given with great love for and knowledge of the specific recipients because their dad & I love them and want to bless them.

The same is true of our Heavenly Father and His good and perfect gifts toward us. God's gifts to us are complete, specifically chosen for us to both bring about our pleasure and to meet our needs. The difference is the wrapping. Sometimes His gifts are wrapped in joy and delight; the sudden bonus we didn't see coming, a peaceful evening with loved ones, the companionship of a dear friend or the contentment of love. Sometimes His gifts are wrapped in sorrow and pain; the battle-weariness of worry about a wayward child, the loss of a loved one, a difficult work environment, sickness or disease. From our highest highs to our lowest lows, God is a good, good Father who gives good and perfect gifts. Each moment of our lives bearing within them the gift of being near to our Father and being transformed, from glory to glory into His likeness upon this earth.

I have written *The Gift* as an invitation for you to sit with your Father and unwrap His good and perfect gifts in your life, and especially in your mission to care for the fatherless and the orphan. We cannot begin this 30-day adventure together without acknowledging that God, in His infinite goodness, has your absolute best in mind, always. You are a priceless treasure and priceless things are most often formed under pressure, through sculpting, and with fire. You are no different. Your life and the totality of your experiences from joy to heartache, are gifts which mold you to God's specific plan for your life and equip you for your unique purpose. Patience doesn't come from peace, it comes from practice. Wisdom isn't automatic, it's sought after and earned.

The Gift is a call to readiness, a call to endurance and a call to intimacy with your Father. Often we enter the journey of foster care and adoption with an understanding that God's heart for the fatherless is reflected all throughout the Bible, so how can we do any(thing) less? One of our most quoted scriptures is James 1:27, "Pure & undefiled religion before God our Father is this: to minister to the orphan and the widow in their distress and to keep oneself unstained by the world." Foster care and adoption all wrapped up in one beautiful passage, ribbons and bows included. So it is there that our expectations sit, in purity and peace, because we what we're doing is sure to be blessed. It's God's favorite thing, pure and undefiled. Right? Well........ Yes. But, wait.

Verse 27 is the *last* verse in James chapter one. To understand a story, we can't start at the last page. We need to turn the pages backward to the beginning, all the way back to verse two. It's in the totality of James' first chapter that we find the completeness of God's gift, this pure and undefiled ministry of caring for the fatherless and the orphan. And this package has your name on it. Not your spouse's name, not your mother's name, not your neighbor's name, and not your children's names... it's for you, about you and for you.

It's time to open *The Gift.*

~Pam Parish~

7

Discussion Questions – Introduction

1. Think about times when you've given gifts. Remember what felt in your heart toward the recipient. Describe those feelings. Can you imagine God feeling the same toward you?

2. As this study begins, Pam points out that God's gifts are good and perfect but they come wrapped in everything from joy to heartache. How does this idea make you feel? Is it difficult for you to consider sorrow and struggle as gifts? Explain why.

3. Read 1 Corinthians 7:7. What does it mean that every man has his own gift? Have you considered your own story and what specific gifts God has given you or is working out in you?

4. What are you specifically asking God to do in your heart and family? How can this group pray for you?

HOW TO USE THIS 30-DAY JOURNAL

TOGETHER

I've written this journal with couples and friends in mind because any journey is easier when there's someone else linking arms with you. If you're married, walk through the thirty days with your spouse. If you're a single parent, find a trusted friend who will challenge you, encourage you, and who isn't afraid to help you dig deep for the truth. You are going to need to rely on each other in your journey. Start now.

REPEATED THEMES

Although no two days of this study are exactly the same, you will see some repeated themes as we travel through the next thirty days. God's mandates regarding the orphan are repeated often in the Bible, so we will revisit them again and again. There are also common areas that cause families to falter and stall. I will repeat them in different ways to make sure you're thinking through potential challenges from every possible angle.

SCRIPTURE STUDY

Each day of *Ready or Not* includes a main scripture and scripture meditations. I encourage you to write down these verses in your personal journal and take time to meditate on them throughout the day. If there's one thing that's most important in this journey, it's the Word written on your heart so you remember it in difficult times. The Word will sustain you, encourage you, give you insight, and bring life and joy into your home. Take all the time you need to meditate on it so it roots deeply into your heart.

JOURNALING

You are going to experience a wide range of emotions, victories, and setbacks. Journaling is a great way to remember and celebrate God's faithfulness. You'll sometimes feel like you're *never* going to get through this challenge or *this* behavior is never going to end, but you will and they do. Being able to look back at the difficulties you've overcome will bring immense encouragement as you move forward.

PRAYER STARTERS

I've given you short prayer starters at the end of each day. These are simply my words—nothing special or sacred. Make them your own. Talk to God about the real stuff that's happening in your heart. This journey is an ongoing conversation between you and God. Be real. Be you. He's waiting to hear from you.

DISCUSSION QUESTIONS

At the end of each day, you'll find a set of questions designed to help you work through and apply the day's devotion. These can be discussed as a couple, in a small group setting, or with a trusted friend. I encourage you to take the time to discuss this material with someone else.

PLACE THESE WORDS ON YOUR HEARTS. GET THEM DEEP INSIDE YOU. TIE THEM

ON YOUR HANDS AND FOREHEADS AS A REMINDER. TEACH THEM TO YOUR

CHILDREN. TALK ABOUT THEM WHEREVER YOU ARE, SITTING AT HOME OR

WALKING IN THE STREET; TALK ABOUT THEM FROM THE TIME YOU GET UP IN

THE MORNING UNTIL YOU FALL INTO BED AT NIGHT. INSCRIBE THEM ON THE

DOORPOSTS AND GATES OF YOUR CITIES SO THAT YOU'LL LIVE A LONG TIME,

AND YOUR CHILDREN WITH YOU, ON THE SOIL THAT GOD PROMISED TO GIVE

YOUR ANCESTORS FOR AS LONG AS THERE IS A SKY OVER THE EARTH.

DEUTERONOMY 11:18-21 (MSG)

FOREWORD

On the small farm where I grew up lived an old mandarin tree. Neat rows of almond trees covered most of the land. But in the very center, a grove of ancient trees tangled with one another – mostly massive cedars and pine. In the middle of the grove, like the tree of life, stood that mandarin.

Its trunk and branches bowed and bent in every direction, like the limbs of an old man. But all winter long, from amidst the black-green leaves, the tree offered little globes of burning gold to anyone with a mind to pluck. And I did, often five or ten a day from December to February.

Once in hand, their peel fell right off. The wedges inside bulged with juice and tangy-sweet flavor. They were a gift straight from Eden. To this day, I can't say I've found anything that tastes better.

That's the kind of fruit I long for my life to yield. To share with every passerby the tangy-sweet savor of grace. To be fully present to the person before me, whether a child my family is fostering or a stranger waiting at the bus stop. To be a patient dad, tender husband, loyal friend. To offer at no charge whatever gift God may choose to grow on my bent branches.

But I'm more aware now than I was as a child what shaped the mandarin tree. Perhaps 100 years of springs and autumns, storms and scorching summers went into that gnarled shape. And through all that, its roots strained ever downward, drawing life year after year from the sandy loam.

Yes, I desire to produce good fruit. But what I tend to want is fruit without the root. I'd love to run a marathon without having to train. Humility without being humbled. Character without scars. A pure heart without the white flames that consume dross.

But it seems God has chosen not to work that way. We'd love for Him to touch us with a shimmering wand, setting us aglow like Cinderella, and suddenly we're nonstop happy-hearted and spilling out grace.

Instead, we trip over unexpected sorrows and unexpected gifts. We receive wounds and then mercifully find them bound. We see our hopes deferred and, on occasion, a hope fulfilled.

These experiences are a, perhaps *the*, primary place of God's work in us. They are roots. And the fruit they produce – or at least the fruit they *may* produce if we open ourselves to what God wants to do – is to be desired beyond all else: steadfastness, wisdom, faith, hope and love…and in the end, what the Bible calls the crown of life.

Pam Parish helps us to feel all of this afresh. As she filters her own poignant memories and confessions and prayers through the first chapter of James, we see with new eyes God's good gifts to us. They hang like burning gold amidst dark green leaves.

Just as important, Pam leads us to the roots beneath this fruit. She tells how things we most wish to avoid can produce the things we most desire. She shows why that marvelous gift of pure religion – to reflect wholeheartedly the love God showed first to us – isn't something we can snatch at the supermarket or even in a Bible study; rather, it must slowly grow from a life rooted deep in Christ.

Perhaps best of all, Pam offers us vivid portraits of what it looks like to open ourselves to all of this. She reminds of the daily choices we can make as ordinary people – foster parents, adoptive moms and dads, husbands and wives and friends.

No, we do not design our lives like architects. We do not construct them like engineers. But we do *participate* with God, as any good farmer does. We cultivate, irrigate, prune as we can…and trust Him for the increase.

As we do, we come to receive, and to bear, God's unparalleled gifts – both to our own joy, and to the good of all who may take shelter beneath our bent branches.

Jedd Medefind

CONSIDER IT PURE JOY, MY BROTHERS AND SISTERS, WHENEVER YOU FACE

TRIALS OF MANY KINDS...

JAMES 1:2

DAY 1: COUNT IT ALL JOY

I'm sitting here this morning meditating on what it means to have joy in the midst of many trials while living the reality of "various trials" along with millions of my fellow Americans. When I write I rarely have the television on because I prefer to write in silence or with worship music quietly playing in the background. This morning is different. The television is my lens into Hurricane Irma's track toward Florida and up the southeast toward Atlanta, the city that I call home. One of our daughters is "riding it out" inland in Jacksonville, Florida and we're cutting a six-day trip to the Smoky Mountains in half so that we can make it back home in time to clear our yard in anticipation of Irma's projected 90mph winds. Millions are displaced from Florida across the southeast. At the same time friends in Houston, TX are cleaning up after Hurricane Harvey roared inland and flooded homes, wiping out hundreds of neighborhoods that may never recover. An 8.0 earthquake shook southern Mexico while much of our North West is on fire.

Hurricanes, floods, earthquakes, fires. Trials of many kinds. Joy? Friends are losing everything, uncertainty looms, and lives are being lost. What about other types of trials? Cancer. Even writing that word brings an overwhelming feeling of sadness in my heart. In the past two years 12 people that I dearly love and admire including both of my parents, a cousin the same age as me and one of my dearest friends in life have all exchanged their earthly addresses for heavenly ones, most because of the "c" word.

Trials of many kinds. Joy? Spouses are gone, children have lost their parents and close friends are no longer here. Finally, what about the trials that are so familiar to those of us walking the "pure and undefiled religion" road of foster care and adoption? Trauma, loss, grief, attachment issues, loneliness, isolation, overwhelming exhaustion, and more. Trials of many kinds. Joy? The sense of helplessness that we feel on many days is so pervasive that it's hard to feel anything but a desire to escape. How do you "count it all joy" in the midst of such great sorrows?

Several years ago I sat with a dear friend whose spouse had been given months to live as a result of cancer. As my friend sat before me weeping tears of great sorrow and fear I said, "Remember that the joy of the Lord is your strength." He looked up at me with eyes full of tears and determination and said, "Oh, I have joy Pam. My joy doesn't depend on how I feel at this very moment." I've never in my life seen a more real display of today's scripture. In that moment joy became clearer to me than ever before. Here sat my friend in a moment of deepest pain and he had joy.

My friend understood, and taught me, in that dark moment what it takes many their entire lives to figure out, if they ever do. Quite simply, joy is not a feeling. It's not an emotion that's given to whimsy or based on the presence of pleasant circumstances. Joy is a knowing; a knowing deep down in our spirit that God is good and, in Him, this trial that is set before us will work out for our good. It's a knowing that in the "work of the ministry" it is an honor to suffer trial and tribulation so that the fruits of His Spirit can be displayed through us for a lost and dying world to see. In this, the display of God's Spirit through us, we find the truth about counting it all a joy when we face trials. This life we've been given, this pure and undefiled religion that we've been called into—friend, it's not about us. It's about Him.

> **"The gift of a Christ-like perspective that for all of us one day, in the blink of an eye, the things of this world will pass away and we will be left with the greatest gift of all, the eternal presence of our Heavenly Father and the eternal joy of one another."**

In hurricanes, floods, earthquakes, and fires we look around and see God's people helping one another, we see people who've lost everything find abundance through friendship, faithfulness of the church community and a physical reminder that 'things' don't matter—people do. It's a gift. The gift of a Christ-like perspective that for all of us one day, in the blink of an eye, the things of this world will pass away and we will be left with the greatest gift of all, the eternal presence of our Heavenly Father and the eternal joy of one another.

Sickness, disease and death bring us together, we lift one another up and we discover God's abiding grace and love. Even through death we are given the gift of an opportunity to point others toward Jesus and turn a moment of deep sorrow into something more meaningful through loving more deeply, living more fully, and choosing joy. This year I've attended memorial services at our church for two giants in God's Kingdom, both whom I dearly loved. In both cases as a 1500 seat auditorium filled with people there to honor lives lived to bring God glory, I watched hands lifted in worship and people who were far from God come back home to Him.

Death, where is your sting? Moments like these take the sting away from heartache. It's hard to imagine your heart being both overwhelmed with sadness and gladness at the same time, but that is exactly how every single person in that room felt, myself included. We said an earthly goodbye to someone we dearly loved, while at the same time experiencing the exceeding peace and joy of the God in whom they had placed their lives. In choosing joy, we acknowledged a life well-lived over an earthly life ending; a life that has now transitioned into the eternally presence of Jesus in heaven. It's a gift. Out of the midst of our darkest moments comes the shining light of Jesus' love bearing within Him the gift of mercy, grace, and joy.

In walking with our kids from hard places through the trials and tribulations of family loss and brokenness, we often discover new friends inside of a community of those navigating the journey of foster care and adoption, we find healing for our own broken places as we seek understanding of the broken places within our kids, and we become willing vessels of God's healing love to a precious, hurting soul. If we can position our hearts and minds toward Jesus in the midst of the never-ending homework, messy rooms, runaway attempts, daily meltdowns, rejection, betrayal and frustrations, we can choose joy in the midst of it all.

Certainly, it's not joyful when your child is screaming curse words at you, threatening you, and rejecting every gesture of love that you give. The joy is in knowing that even so, it is well with your soul. Even in "this" God is near. In the midst of the trial, He is still good and you are still His beloved child in whom He is well pleased. It's a gift. The gift of leaning on Him, trusting Him, choosing joy in Him and becoming more like Him during the most hurtful moments of life.

There's an old German saying, "You cannot prevent the birds from flying over your head, but you can prevent them from making nests in your hair." In the same way, you cannot prevent trials and tribulations from occurring in your life whether it be walking with children from hard places, death and disease, or natural disasters, but you can prevent them from stealing your joy and knocking you off course. In this way we count it all a joy when we face trials of many kinds.

The gift of joy is that no matter your circumstance, you can tilt your face toward heaven and feel the warmth of your Father's love and pleasure with you. Choose joy.

Scripture Meditation: Take a few moments to read the following Scriptures. Allow the Holy Spirit to speak to your heart about each of them.

> **Matthew 6:13** "And lead us not into temptation, but deliver us from the evil one."
>
> **2 Timothy 2:3** "Endure suffering along with me, as a good soldier of Christ Jesus."
>
> **1 Corinthians 10:13** "The temptations in your life are no different from what others experience. And God is faithful. He will not allow the temptation to be more than you can stand. When you are tempted, he will show you a way out so that you can endure."
>
> **1 Peter 1:6** "So be truly glad. There is wonderful joy ahead, even though you must endure many trials for a little while."

Romans 5:3 "We can rejoice, too, when we run into problems and trials, for we know that they help us develop endurance."

Capturing Thoughts: Throughout your scripture journey, I encourage you to capture your thoughts, fears, moments of joy, memories, and challenges. It will be a great encouragement to go back and read what you've written. Looking back, you'll be surprised how much you and your family grow throughout your experiences.

Prayer Starter: Father, today we choose joy and we choose to see your goodness, mercy and grace even in the midst of our trial. Give us the ability to see beyond the immediate circumstance as we look upward toward you, as we trust you for your wisdom and direction. Thank you for calling us to this gift of your grace called foster care and adoption. Help us to be the reflection of you that you would have us to be for our children, our community and the world around us.

Discussion Questions – Day 1: Count it All Joy

1. When you think about the concepts of trial and joy as it relates to your foster care and adoption experience, what is the most challenging aspect?

2. Today's devotion says, "If we can position our hearts and minds toward Jesus in the midst of the never-ending homework, messy rooms, runaway attempts, daily meltdowns, rejection, betrayal and frustrations, we can choose joy in the midst of it all." Talk about how you navigate the difficulties of parenting in your family. How can you work on choosing joy, even when you're tired and frustrated?

3. Read 1 Corinthians 10:13. What do you think it means that your temptations aren't any different from the temptations that others face?

4. What are your biggest fears in this situation? Take time to put words to them—in writing, in conversation, or in prayer—so that they are exposed to the light and not hidden in darkness.

My Journey:

(Use this space to capture your thoughts, prayers, concerns and questions)

DAY 2: TESTING OF FAITH

You've stayed up too late every night, texting with your friends, binging on the latest Netflix show, or any activity other than studying. Today is test day. It's the big one too. You're totally unprepared. As you slide into your seat mentally beating yourself up for not being better prepared, your teacher's voice rings out across the classroom, "I've decided that today's test will count as a practice test since many of you need a little more time to master the concepts that we've been reviewing." Instant relief. You've been saved. As the teacher passes the test around, you joyfully take yours knowing that it will reveal the areas where you need to grow so that you're ready when the *real* test comes. The tests of our faith are practice tests that prepare us from test-to-test for the inevitable trials that God knows are before us, all designed to show us areas in which we need to grow so that we're ready to be found faithful and true on that day when we stand before Him in glory—the Final Exam.

I can feel the emotions rising in my chest and the tears stinging the back of my eyes as I consider many of the times that my faith has been tested. Those "rubber meets the road" moments when the circumstance in front of me felt insurmountable or hopeless. Those moments that required me to turn heavenward with tear-stained cheeks, clenched fists, and tattered emotions to choose a direction for my tired mind and frayed faith.

There have been many seasons and challenges in my life that have forced me to confront the weakness of the faith within my own heart. I remember reading the book of Job in a desperate season and feeling, really feeling, what Job felt as he watched the life he loved shatter around him and wondered what he did to cause it. He was simply serving the Lord, righteously. He was raising his family to serve and love the Lord. He was loving his neighbor. Yet, it all came crashing down. I understand his broken and unsure heart. I've also heard the voice of the enemy question, "Where is your God now?!?" when the situation is grim and hope seems lost, even though we've done our absolute best for the right reasons. And, I've confronted the demons of my own desires as they've tempted me to quit, give up, and walk away because - this... *it's just too much. I don't deserve it.*

What is it about this journey of pure and undefiled religion—ministry to the fatherless—that brings with it so much testing and turmoil? It's holiness. A holiness that endures on behalf of another. A holiness that goes to the Cross, even though He did nothing to deserve it. Our hearts cry out to be *"more like Him,"* to be transformed into His likeness, to love like He first loved us, and to walk in His miraculous power. Even as those prayers cross our lips and extend beyond our uplifted hands, our imaginations play a comfortable and soothing movie in our minds of grateful people helped by our generosity, goodness, and kindness. We consciously and subconsciously believe

> **"What is it about this journey of pure and undefiled religion—ministry to the fatherless—that brings with it so much testing and turmoil? It's holiness. A holiness that endures on behalf of another."**

that "*more like Him*" is comfortable and easy. It's a lie whispered to us by the enemy of our souls to create discontent within our hearts and draw us away from the Truth.

The Truth is that love went to the Cross. Love laid down His desire in the Garden of Gethsemane as He sweated great drops of blood and asked His Father to remove this suffering from before Him, yet yielded Himself to the will of His Father despite the agony that lay before Him. This journey of pure and undefiled religion—ministry to the fatherless—is not about us helping *them*. It's not about what God can do *through* us *for* an orphan. It's about what God can do *in* us because of our obedience to His Word and reliance upon Him. This current trial, this suffering, this heartbreak, this desperate need for Jesus to intervene… it's about you, and me. It has nothing to do with them.

"Father, if you are willing, take this cup from me; yet not my will, but Yours be done." Jesus (Luke 22:42)

Testing will grow our faith like weight training will grow our muscles. Our life on this earth as we seek to be "*more like Him*" should be a continual progression of "faith training," strengthening our mind, will, and emotions in Him so that when trials are upon us we have the patient perseverance required to allow His purpose to be displayed, despite our discomfort. As my husband and I have parented our daughters and sought to love them regardless of love's messiness, we've continually found our faith tested and our pride exposed.

I don't want my daughters to suffer.
I don't want my daughters to make poor choices that will impact their lives.

I want my daughters to be happy.

I want my daughters to serve and love Jesus.

I want Jesus to know my daughter's names on the day that they each stand before Him.

I. I. I. I. I. And the list could go on. As I typed these sentences I could hear Joyce Meyer's voice in my head and visualize her marching around the stage mimicking a robot repeating, "What about me? What about me? What about me?" We are selfish. It's baked into our sin nature. We must learn to flip the script that our own desires write and look at the Author of our lives and trust His version of the story. The story that He is writing in our children's lives, and ours, is for His glory and our refinement. It's about redemption, it's about love, it's about holiness.

The gift of testing is endurance—a patient perseverance that requires our eyes to be focused on the finish line of eternity. It requires us to continue through the discomfort, joyfully endure many trials, and fix our eyes on Jesus, the Author and Finisher of our Faith. As we pass each test, our faith is strengthened for the next, onward and onward until we see Him face-to-face.

Scripture Meditation: Take a few moments to read the following Scriptures. Allow the Holy Spirit to speak to your heart about each of them.

> **Matthew 16:24-26** "Then Jesus told his disciples, 'If any of you wants to be my follower, you must give up your own way, take up your cross, and follow me. If you try to hang on to your life, you will lose it. But if you give up your life for my sake, you will save it. And what do you benefit if you gain the whole earth but lose your soul? Is anything

worth more than your soul?"

Malachi 3:3 "He will sit like a refiner of silver, burning away the dross. He will purify the Levites, refining them like gold and silver, so that they may once again offer acceptable sacrifices to the Lord."

2 Timothy 1:9 "He has saved us and called us to a holy life—not because of anything we have done but because of his own purpose and grace. This grace was given us in Christ Jesus before the beginning of time."

1 Peter 3:17 "It is better, if God should will it so, that you suffer for doing what is right rather than for doing what is wrong."

Capturing Thoughts: Throughout your adoption journey, I encourage you to capture your thoughts, fears, moments of joy, memories, and challenges. It will be a great encouragement to go back and read what you've written before. Looking back, you'll be surprised how much you and your family grow through your experiences.

Prayer Starter: Father, I feel so weak. I know the testing of my faith produces endurance so that I can stand against the things to come in the future. Right now, I'm feeling like I can't even endure today. I invite you to guide me in wisdom, to correct me in my understanding, and to challenge me in my walk with you. Thank you for teaching me to trust in you, regardless of my circumstances.

Discussion Questions – Day 2: Testing of Faith

1. Have you ever reached a place where, as Pam describes, you have been tempted to quit, give up and walk away because - *this... it's just too much. I don't deserve it.*? How did you make it through? How did the test of

endurance change your relationship with God?

2. Read Matthew 16:24-26. Jesus makes it clear that to be His follower, we must give up our own way, take up our cross, and follow Him. What does this scripture mean to you? In what ways are you trying to hang on to your own way?

3. How does the idea that the testing of your faith is meant to build spiritual endurance help you in your struggle?

4. What is one thing you can do this week to make going through the trial easier?

My Journey:

(Use this space to capture your thoughts, prayers, concerns and questions)

So, LET IT GROW, FOR WHEN YOUR ENDURANCE (PATIENCE) IS FULLY
DEVELOPED, YOU WILL BE PERFECT AND COMPLETE, NEEDING NOTHING.

JAMES 1:4

DAY 3: PATIENCE MADE PERFECT

"I don't know how much more that I can take. I feel like throwing in the towel. The winds of fear have caused my faith to shake. You're the only One to help me now. Cause everything I said that I believe is tested by this adversity. Well I don't know how or I don't know when, but I know your peace will reign." There's no telling how many times that these opening words to my friend Danny Chambers' song *Overwhelmed* have played as the soundtrack to my heart's desperate cry for an answer, an end or just a break.

We can all think of days that have stretched us far beyond what we thought we could bear and as we fall into bed at night we think, "Whew. I'm so glad that is over." But what happens when those days stretch into years with no end in sight? A drug addicted child. A child who rages. A child who hates you, and wants nothing to do with being a part of your family. How do you hold it together through it all without throwing in the towel?

There's a famous quote that Bilbo says in Lord of the Rings, Fellowship of the Ring when describing to Frodo why he left The Shire to retire in Rivendale. He says, "I feel thin, sort of stretched, like butter scraped over too much bread." I've quoted that line to my husband on more days than I can count because I've never heard a phrase that so accurately describes what I feel like when it's taking everything inside of me to hold myself together, and at the same time be what I need to be for a child (or several) who is going through a challenging and exhausting season.

In the "thin" place where your emotions are raw, exhaustion is heavy and your patience is worn, it's easy to justify quitting and giving up. Excuses like, "I'm not helping them anyway." "I just need to get back to my old self." "I can't do any more than I'm already doing." "They don't want to be a part of this family." And many others crowd our minds and tempt our hearts. This is why you'll find the word "patience" and "endurance" interchanged in different versions of today's scripture. Because it's not easy, it takes effort and focus to keep moving, and to wait.

What I have found in myself as I've walked through these seasons and have come out on the other side of some, and am still praying through and waiting on others, is that my patience/endurance has indeed developed. What once would freak me out and send me into a panic, now sends me to

> **"What once would freak me out and send me into a panic, now sends me to my knees in prayer."**

my knees in prayer. The reaction to lash out at a child for what "you are doing to me" has been replaced with an empathy and patience that allows me to see her in her own struggle and move "me" out of the way to trust God with His hand for her. The beauty of sitting next to or waiting on a child who is in the midst of "stuff" in his or her life and loving him or her in spite of it is a gift. It's a gift I didn't have inside of me ten years ago when this journey began. It's the gift of me being complete in me, needing nothing "from" them to make me whole, because I am complete outside of their behaviors, words and actions toward me, or otherwise.

As I've walked through difficulty and hurt with my children from hard places, I have found my patience has grown to allow them to walk out their stories, whatever their choices, without allowing the enemy to beat me up or blame-shift. My job is simply to love, and trust God. To wait and allow the gift of patience within me to have its full work so that I'm left perfect and complete, needing nothing. The truth is, it's not my kids' job to fulfill me. Only Jesus can do that.

Scripture Meditation: Take a few moments to read the following Scriptures. Allow the Holy Spirit to speak to your heart about each of them.

> **Romans 5:3-4** "We can rejoice, too, when we run into problems and trials, for we know that they help us develop endurance. And endurance develops strength of character, and character strengthens our confident hope of salvation."

> **Galatians 6:9** "So let's not get tired of doing what is good. At just the right time we will reap a harvest of blessing if we don't give up."

> **Colossians 1:11-12** "We also pray that you will be strengthened with all his glorious power so you will have all the endurance and patience you need. May you be filled with joy always thanking the Father. He has enabled you to share in the inheritance that belongs to his people who live in the light."

> **Psalm 27:34** "Put your hope in the Lord. Travel steadily along his path. He will honor you by giving you the land. You will see the wicked destroyed."

Capturing Thoughts: Throughout your adoption journey, I encourage you to capture your thoughts, fears, moments of joy, memories, and challenges. It will be a great encouragement to go back and read what you've written before. Looking back, you'll be surprised how much you and your family grow through your experiences.

Prayer Starter: Lord, I want to be perfect and complete in you, lacking and needing nothing from an earthly perspective. My heart knows this is where I need to be, but this is so hard. Help me learn to trust you and not to take things into my own hands or worry about them in my own heart. Give me the ability to give to my children what they need because I've first received from you what I need.

Discussion Questions – Day 3: Patience Made Perfect

1. Have you ever been too afraid to pray about a situation because you know you're handling it all wrong? Why do you think it's so difficult to trust God, especially when we're in really murky waters with our kids and family?

2. Today's devotion says, "In the 'thin' place where your emotions are raw, exhaustion is heavy and your patience is worn, it's easy to justify quitting or giving up." Talk about a time you've felt your emotions were in a 'thin' place. Did you give up? Why or why not?

3. Read Romans 5:3-4. Why do you think testing and trial help us to develop stronger character? What are some character traits you have today that are a result of trials you endured long ago?

4. How do you see your patience growing as you walk out your family's story of foster care and adoption? Take time to celebrate those areas of growth that you are already seeing.

My Journey:

(Use this space to capture your thoughts, prayers, concerns and questions)

IF YOU NEED WISDOM, ASK OUR GENEROUS GOD, AND HE WILL GIVE IT TO YOU.

HE WILL NOT REBUKE YOU FOR ASKING.

JAMES 1:5

DAY 4: WISDOM

Like many of you reading these words, I started this journey woefully unprepared for what would be ahead of me. We thought we were providing family to children who didn't have anyone else, and even though we knew it wouldn't be easy, we kind of expected that after a couple of months of adjustment things would level out. You know, just "be" family - comfortable and "regular." We truthfully didn't know what we didn't know. We were ignorant about trauma, loss, and the types of behaviors that children from hard places could exhibit as a result of their stunted development due to abuse and neglect.

Because of our ignorance we were blindsided by things like defiant behavior, running away, sexual acting out, cutting, lying, poor school performance, and more. We felt overwhelmed and scared of complete and total failure. I remember begging God to show me the way to help. It was at a very low point in our family that I decided to attend my first Christian Alliance for Orphans (CAFO) Summit. It was in Nashville and I attended so that I could gather the information to start an Orphan Care ministry at our church effectively. My attendance wasn't even focused on me, or our family's personal situation. I was attending all of the ministry-related sessions to figure out how to "do the ministry" of orphan care well in a church setting, not even considering that "the ministry" of caring for the those in my own home was crumbling.

35

As I was looking for a session, I found myself turned around and lost, not able to find the room it was in. In the process I walked by the main auditorium, it was full of people there for another session. On stage was this woman with stunning grey hair speaking. Giving up on my intended session, I walked in and sat down. The woman speaking was Dr. Karyn Purvis, author of The Connected Child and co-founder of TCU's Institute for Child Development. She was talking about trauma and brain development in children from hard places who've experienced abuse and neglect. As she talked, she described what was going on in my home as if she had a hidden video camera capturing my children's thoughts, behaviors, and history. I was dumbfounded and transformed. It was at that moment that I knew what I hadn't previously known - what my children were experiencing, and *doing*, was NORMAL for kids who've experienced trauma. AND there was a way to HEAL and change it!!!! Through this accidental session, the Lord graciously answered my heart's cry for wisdom. I sat in stunned silence with tears streaming down my face for 30 minutes after the session was finished.

Following that session, I devoured everything I could get my hands on from Dr. Purvis, and in the process, discovered Empowered to Connect (ETC), a curriculum for foster and adoptive parents based on TCU's *Trust Based Relational Intervention* (TBRI) principles. My husband and I flew to Dallas and were trained as ETC facilitators two months after I accidentally sat in Dr. Purvis' session. That moment transformed our parenting and it transformed my life. It was the wisdom that I didn't know I needed but God gave me generously, without rebuking me or chastising me for not knowing.

Before TBRI and ETC, we made a ton of mistakes in our parenting. Many times making the problem worse rather than better because of our ignorance. Yet even in our mess, God heard our prayer for understanding and wisdom, and He answered it. We need wisdom to navigate this journey with our kids. I've learned to ask for wisdom specifically every single day, in every situation. That simple and purposeful prayer has led to more chance encounters, random conversations, and resource discoveries than I could tell you about. Ask for wisdom. You cannot do this without God's divine intervention to direct you to the right places, at the right time for the right information. The knowledge that I've gained is a gift that has allowed me to be faithful in walking with my kids in their stuff, and even helping other families do the same.

> **"Yet, even in our mess, God heard our prayer for understanding and wisdom, and He answered it."**

Scripture Meditation: Take a few moments to read the following Scriptures. Allow the Holy Spirit to speak to your heart about each of them.

Proverbs 1:5 "Let the wise listen to these proverbs and become even wiser. Let those with understanding receive guidance."

Proverbs 2:1-5 "My child, listen to what I say and treasure my commands. Tune your ears to wisdom, and concentrate on understanding. Cry out for insight, and ask for understanding. Search for them as you would for silver; seek them like hidden treasures. Then you will understand what it means to fear the Lord, and you will gain knowledge of God."

Proverbs 8:11 "For wisdom is far more valuable than rubies. Nothing you desire can compare with it."

Proverbs 19:20 "Get all the advice and instruction you can, so you will be wise the rest of your life."

Capturing Thoughts: Throughout your adoption journey, I encourage you to capture your thoughts, fears, moments of joy, memories, and challenges. It will be a great encouragement to go back and read what you've written before. Looking back, you'll be surprised how much you and your family grow through your experiences.

Prayer Starter: Lord, we need wisdom. There's so much about our children's pasts that we do not know. There's so much about our own habits, behaviors and responses that we still are learning how to manage and shift. Will you bring us the right resources, people and understanding so that we can successfully accomplish all that you've put into our lives for your glory and our own good?

Discussion Questions – Day 4: Wisdom

1. Today's devotion challenges us to ask the Lord for wisdom and trust Him in the areas where we are the most unprepared. Why is it sometimes hard to admit that we need to learn more?

2. Read Proverbs 19:20. Discuss how advice and instruction can help you grow in the area of fostering and adoption.

3. Talk about the types of things you feel like you could use greater understanding and wisdom around. Share ideas on how you can look for resources and training.

4. Have there been times that you've made a problem worse, simply because you didn't have all of the information or proper training? Describe how you overcame that obstacle and corrected course.

My Journey:

(Use this space to capture your thoughts, prayers, concerns and questions)

BUT WHEN YOU ASK HIM, BE SURE THAT YOUR FAITH IS IN GOD ALONE.

JAMES 1:6A

DAY 5: WITHOUT A DOUBT

Yesterday we established that God wants you to ask for wisdom and he will give it to you, without rebuke. The only thing he requires of us when granting us wisdom is to trust Him, and Him alone. When God brought me the understanding of what was happening to our girls because of their trauma we changed everything about the way we approached their behaviors and our responses. There were many critics of the ways in which we shifted our family's response to behavior and consequence; everyone has an opinion about discipline and tolerance. Regardless of anyone else's opinion, we had to trust God and His voice and direction over the voice and direction of everyone else around us. Following God's specific wisdom for our circumstances required total faith in Him, and Him alone.

> "There were many critics of the ways in which we shifted our family's response to behavior and consequence; everyone has an opinion about discipline and tolerance."

I often imagine Noah as he and his family were building the ark. The community around him thought he had lost his mind. What he was doing was ridiculous. God had given him wisdom—an understanding of what was to come and exactly how to protect his family and fulfill God's assignment. It took him approximately 70 years to build the ark. 70 years of sneers and remarks from his neighbors. 70 years of questioning and doubt. 70 years without rain from the sky. Can you imagine how difficult it was for Noah and his family to hold on to the wisdom that God had given them on the building of the ark and the coming flood in the midst of intense doubt and criticism?

How long are you going to put up with *that behavior*?
Are you sure you're doing the right thing?
What about the rest of your family?
Are you a glutton for punishment?

All of these questions, and many more, were asked of us as our family grew from a family of three to a family of 10, now a family of 17 (and counting) with sons-in-laws and grandkids. Each question forced us to defend our faith in God and what we felt like He was guiding us to do as a family. Each behavior or crisis stood as evidence against us in the eyes of our critics that what we were doing was a mistake. Each question challenged the wisdom of God that He had given us concerning our family. Each one an opportunity to trust God, and Him alone, and lovingly guide our friends into an understanding of this unique calling that God has placed upon our heart to care for the fatherless, and be with them in their distress.

As our family grew and the challenges of parenting so many kids with complex trauma and loss grew along with it, we had to be absolutely sure that we were following God's design and not our own desires. That assurance came simply—in our minds and hearts there just wasn't another option. My husband and I were in complete and total agreement. The guiding factor for us was always the question from Isaiah 6:7, Then I heard the Lord asking, "Whom should I send as a messenger to this people? Who will go for us?" I said, "Here I am. Send me." Having that assurance and understanding, we were now required to ask God for the wisdom to walk out His Call on our lives and then to follow through by acting on His guidance and trusting Him completely.

God will faithfully guide and direct you in your specific family, around your specific children. He will grant you the exact wisdom that you need through resources, through others who've traveled this road ahead of you and through His Word. Your job is to trust Him, and Him alone, and to act upon the wisdom He is granting you in faith and obedience, just like Noah did. You cannot do the work of caring for the fatherless without intimacy and trust in your Heavenly Father. You absolutely must cry out for wisdom and trust in Him. It is a life-changing gift to us that we have a Heavenly Father who is trustworthy and true to His word.

Scripture Meditation: Take a few moments to read the following Scriptures. Allow the Holy Spirit to speak to your heart about each of them.

Psalm 3:4 "I call out to the Lord, and He answers me from his holy mountain."

Psalm 31:14-15 "But I trust in you, Lord; I say, 'You are my God,' My times are in your hands; deliver me from the hands of my enemies, from those who pursue me."

Proverbs 3:5-8 "Trust in the Lord with all your heart and lean not on your own understanding; in all your ways submit to Him, and He will make your paths straight. Do not be wise in your own eyes; fear the Lord and shun evil. This will bring health to your body and nourishment to your bones."

Proverbs 29:25 "Fear of man will prove to be a snare, but whoever trusts in the Lord is kept safe."

Capturing Thoughts: Throughout your adoption journey, I encourage you to capture your thoughts, fears, moments of joy, memories, and challenges. It will be a great encouragement to go back and read what you've written before. Looking back, you'll be surprised how much you and your family grow through your experiences.

Prayer Starter: Jesus, we trust in you, and in you alone. Forgive us for times that we've trusted our own abilities or understanding above you. Forgive us for times we've trusted in experts or others, instead of turning to you. We know you are guiding us and that as we walk in obedience to your calling in our lives, you will direct our steps and clear our path.

Discussion Questions – Day 5: Without a Doubt

1. What doubts are you struggling with right now? Be honest with yourself, and with the Lord about where your doubts and fears are. He alone can help you remove them.

2. Take time to evaluate the voices in your life and in your family's story. Are they voices that reflect and uphold the call of God for you? Or, are they voices that speak doubt and fear?

3. Proverbs 29:25 talks about fear of man being a snare. Talk about ways you've allowed fear of man to hinder you. Discuss how you can trusts the Lord more in these situations.

4. Consider the story of Noah that Pam shared. Do you often feel like people think you're crazy for the choices you've made in growing your family? If so, how can you handle these feelings better in light of today's devotional?

My Journey:

(Use this space to capture your thoughts, prayers, concerns and questions)

DO NOT WAVER, FOR A PERSON WITH DIVIDED LOYALTY IS AS UNSETTLED AS A
WAVE OF THE SEA THAT IS BLOWN AND TOSSED BY THE WIND.

JAMES 1:6B

DAY 6: TOSSED BY THE WIND

What God asks of us within our individual walks of faith is simple—trust.
Trust in His Word and in the direction that He's given us in our lives, in
every moment. Yet, somehow we've gotten the idea that if that thing that
we've "felt like" God was telling us doesn't look like or turn out like what
we "think" it should, that it's okay to figure out something different so that
we can restore our comfort level and our easy idea of what it means to do
God's will. We KNOW that God spoke to us about *this* child but now that
we're here and it's hard, we're not sure.

Right here in the second part of verse six James turns extremely serious. So
far we know not to expect that things will be entirely easy and that we
should be joyful in trial, we know there are going to be tests of our faith, we
understand that patience will have its perfect work, we know that God will
give us wisdom if we ask for it, and we need to trust in Him alone. So far—
so good, but right here in the closing of verse six James says, "I need you to
listen up, this is serious. It's time to think about what you're committing to
and make sure you mean it." Right here, James would say to us, "Wait. You
asked God for this child, you begged and pleaded with Him to work this
situation out. You felt like mountains were moved to get this child into your
home. Yet now that it's hard and you are unsure of yourself, you think you
heard God wrong? Hold up. Do not waver."

It's often here, right at the place where we realize that what God has called us to do, those prayers that He's faithfully answered and those dreams that we've dreamed which have come true are going to require something more of us than we ever imagined. It's in this place that we start to waver and question ourselves, and ultimately God. Instead of trusting God and His Word, we ask our friends for their advice. Instead of reminding ourselves of the miracles that worked together to get us to this moment, we focus on the uncertainty of the moment and forget all that God has done.

The gift that James is giving us here as he takes a hard turn to close out this verse is brutal honesty. You can't trust God yet take the advice of your friends over His Word. You can't have your faith in God alone at the same time that you're rehearsing your doubt with your spouse every single night. We cannot allow ourselves to be tossed back and forth by the wind of our emotions and opinions of our friends or family. Do not waver in the faith that brought you to this moment.

> **"The gift that James is giving us here as he takes a hard turn to close out this verse is brutal honesty. You can't trust God yet take the advice of your friends over His Word."**

I'll close by this quote from Pastor Greg Boyd, "Biblical faith isn't about trying to attain certainty; it's about committing to a course of action in the face of uncertainty." When we've given our commitment to God, and to our children, to walk with them for the rest of our life—no matter what—we must be keepers of our word, and His. The gift that God gives us in the midst of that commitment is the opportunity to put unwavering faith into action and trust in Him—no matter what. Do not waver.

Scripture Meditation: Take a few moments to read the following Scriptures. Allow the Holy Spirit to speak to your heart about each of them.

> **Isaiah 40:31** "But those who trust in the Lord will find new strength. They will soar high on wings like eagles. They will run and not grow weary. They will walk and not faint."

> **Colossians 3:2** "Think about the things of heaven, not the things of earth."

> **Deuteronomy 4:9** "But watch out! Be careful never to forget what you yourself have seen. Do not let these memories escape from your mind as long as you live! And be sure to pass them on to your children and grandchildren."

> **John 10:10** "The thief's purpose is to steal and kill and destroy. My purpose is to give them a rich and satisfying life."

Capturing Thoughts: Throughout your adoption journey, I encourage you to capture your thoughts, fears, moments of joy, memories, and challenges. It will be a great encouragement to go back and read what you've written before. Looking back, you'll be surprised how much you and your family grow through your experiences.

Prayer Starter: Lord, there are so many voices. Help me to navigate my fearful thoughts, my anxious heart, and my failed humanity. Give me the wisdom to hear your voice alone and to place your direction for my faith and family above every other thought, opinion or feeling—mine or from another person.

Discussion Questions – Day 6: Tossed by the Wind

1. When you think about the theme of today's devotion, *tossed by the wind*, what feelings does it bring up in you? Can you identify the opposing emotions or opinions?

2. Read Deuteronomy 4:9. Talk about the opposing opinions that can sometimes toss your emotions and faith back and forth. How does this verse and its reminder to remember the truth of the goodness and faithfulness of the Lord help you to calm your inner storm?

3. Pam quotes Pastor Greg Boyd, "Biblical faith isn't about trying to attain certainty; it's about committing to a course of action in the face of uncertainty." Write down some uncertainties that you're struggling with and openly pray through those with God, and if possible with a trusted faith-filled friend.

4. Take a minute to talk about how God led you into this relationship with your child. Do you remember His goodness in the beginning? Talk about what led you into this journey and why you feel God chose you for this child at this time.

My Journey:

(Use this space to capture your thoughts, prayers, concerns and questions)

DAY 7: WHEN GOD IS SILENT

Silence. It's that precious gift that we, as parents, often dream about—just five straight minutes of silence would feel like a miracle. Silence is a gift that we often yearn for, until it's silence from God. It feels like the farthest thing from a gift when we reach those seasons that we're desperately crying out for God to answer us, to change the situation (or our child) and we hear nothing. We become angry and are tempted to rely on our own resources and reasoning. Stop. This is where, as believers, we get ourselves into trouble.

I once heard a pastor say, "When God is silent, you need to go back to the last thing you heard Him say and keep being faithful until there's a breakthrough. God hasn't changed His mind, and you shouldn't change course." It's truth. As an adoptive or foster parent, there's a profound

> **"As an adoptive or foster parent, there's a profound sense of God's purpose that many would classify as a "calling" upon our lives."**

sense of God's purpose that many would classify as a "calling" upon our lives. We feel like He has led us into this and spoken to us about the specific children that He has placed into our care. Yet we find ourselves crying out to Him in the midst of our struggle in the hard places with our children from hard places. If we really stop right here to examine our heart, and our request of God, most of the time we're begging Him to remove us *from* the difficulty rather than trusting Him to navigate us *through* it.

It's exactly the place that the nation of Israel found itself in after they heard God's promise to take them out of slavery and into a land flowing with milk and honey. It's the place that they found themselves at after they had experienced the parting of the Red Sea, literal manna from heaven, a visible cloud for guidance during the day and a pillar of fire by night. It's exactly the place they were, on the verge of the promise, when walking into God's promise seemed too much for them to bear, too scary, too overwhelming, and outside of their capacity to navigate. So they complained, doubted and talked amongst themselves—believing the negative report of fearful human spies over the Word of the Lord who performed miracles to deliver them to this place.

In Numbers Chapter 14:26-38, God lays out the consequences of their doubt—death of the dream. They would never see the Promised Land in their lifetimes. Instead the promise would be delivered to their children. They would dwell in the wilderness, stuck at the very mountain they were desperate to escape until a whole generation died. God's promise was true, His Word would come to pass but they would not see it because they had chosen to focus on the obstacles in their path instead of the obstacle remover on their side.

The Lord performed miracles far beyond what we might ever know to bring our children into our care. He did it for one reason only—so that they might know Him and love Him. So that, through Him, their wounds could be bound up and their hearts healed. That promise to our kids will come to pass. It's up to us whether we're around to see it is fulfilled.

The distance from where you are right now to the manifestation of that promise is known only to God. Doubting and divided loyalty will always lead us to running in place until we turn again to faith in Him and not focus on our circumstance. The gift that God is giving us in His silence is an opportunity for perseverance to, again, have its perfect work in our lives by trusting Him and staying firm where He planted us.

Scripture Meditation: Take a few moments to read the following Scriptures. Allow the Holy Spirit to speak to your heart about each of them.

> **Psalm 68:5-6** "Father to the fatherless, defender of widows—this God, whose dwelling is holy. God places the lonely in families; he sets the prisoners free and gives them joy. But he makes the rebellious live in a sun-scorched land."

> **Numbers 14:26-38** *Read aloud from your Bible.*

> **Romans 12:20** "Instead, do what the Scriptures say: 'If your enemies are hungry, feed them. If they are thirsty, give them something to drink, and they will be ashamed of what they have done to you."

> **Colossians 3:12-13** "Since God chose you to be the holy people whom he loves, you must clothe yourselves with tenderhearted mercy, kindness, humility, gentleness, and patience. You must make allowance for each other's faults and forgive the person who offends you. Remember the Lord forgave you, so you must forgive others."

Capturing Thoughts: Throughout your adoption journey, I encourage you to capture your thoughts, fears, moments of joy, memories, and challenges. It will be a great encouragement to go back and read what you've written before. Looking back, you'll be surprised how much you and your family grow through your experiences.

Prayer Starter: Father, give me the ability to see beyond the mountain that's in front of me and to trust you. In times when I am desperate for your voice, remind me to stand in faith and obedience to the last thing that you've said to me and trust you for the outcome. Forgive me for doubt or double-mindedness.

Discussion Questions – Day 7: When God is Silent

1. Have you ever experienced the silence of God? Talk about what it felt like and what it took for you to persevere.

2. Today's devotion says, "…we find ourselves crying out to Him in the midst of our struggle in the hard places with our children from hard places. If we really stop right here to examine our heart, and our request of God, most of the time we're begging Him to remove us *from* the difficulty rather than trusting Him to navigate us *through* it. " In what ways does that challenge you? Can you imagine a different approach to prayer and wisdom in these moments?

3. Talk about a time that you wanted God to rescue you from a situation and He didn't. What happened? How did you grow?

4. What are some specific areas of breakthrough that you're needing from God right now? How can this group be of help to you?

My Journey:

(Use this space to capture your thoughts, prayers, concerns and questions)

DAY 8: DOUBLE-MINDED INSTABILITY

Stability is the very thing that we set out to provide for the children that God brings into our care and our homes through foster care and adoption. Yet it is this very thing that the enemy of our souls will use to try and wreck our family and alter God's design for us and for our children. We become unstable when we allow the promises of God and His Word to take a backseat to the future-casting of our friends and the power of their words in our life.

We've pretty much heard it all...

"Are you crazy?"

"Have you lost your minds?"

"What are you doing to your kids?"

"Are you sure you can handle it?"

"You really shouldn't have to put up with that kind of behavior."

"If I were you, I would _____."

"What if they _____?"

You get the point. Have you ever heard the phrase, "Opinions are like belly buttons, everyone has one"? That's how we need to consider these types of statements. I'm sure they mean well, in most cases at least. For you and me this is dangerous and shaky ground though. The simple truth is that our friends and family don't answer to God for our calling. Only we do. Other people's opinions aren't going to stand as witness to our faithfulness to God and His guidance, more times than not they will stand as evidence against us, testifying to our lack of faith and divided loyalty.

Some of the most heartbreaking seasons of my life have been those when I've battled to understand the wisdom of God against the loud and seemingly understanding thoughts and opinions of my friends and family. In most cases their thoughts were solicited by me as I relayed a story of a struggling daughter and tried to decide what the right course of action would be on our part. In the process I would find myself sometimes being more harsh than necessary, or the opposite - too lenient where solid correction was needed. It breaks my heart because in the process my actions and words caused harm because they weren't seasoned with the salt of love, but instead with bitterness, exhaustion, and frustration. As I've grown in faith and experience, the Lord has certainly taught me to remain calm and give situations time to allow me to calm down and discuss it with Him before responding. Trust me, this isn't easy for me. I don't do well with waiting to address something that's bothering me. However I've found that in doing so, my actions and words line up with Him, and the situations resolve themselves much more quickly and peacefully.

> **"As I've grown in faith and experience, the Lord has certainly taught me to remain calm and give situations time to allow myself to calm down and discuss it with Him before responding."**

The enemy will tempt and test you to divide your heart and your thinking in order to keep you off balance and create instability in your home. Learning to discern Godly wisdom from human opinions will only happen as you immerse yourself in His Word and keep your feet and mind firmly planted on Him.

We cannot allow what someone else thinks or does hold more power over our decisions and family than what God says to do in His Word. We are to hold fast to the promises that He gave us in the beginning, refuse to doubt, and count it a joy in trial. The gift of stability in God's direction for your family is a surety of your next step and a peace that prevails, regardless of your circumstances.

Scripture Meditation: Take a few moments to read the following Scriptures. Allow the Holy Spirit to speak to your heart about each of them.

2 Samuel 22:31-32 "As for God, his way is perfect: The Lord's word is flawless; he shields all who take refuge in him. For who is God besides the Lord? And who is the Rock except our God?"

Proverbs 3:5-8 "Trust in the Lord with all your heart, and lean not on your own understanding; in all your ways acknowledge Him, and He shall direct your paths. Do not be wise in your own eyes; fear the Lord and depart from evil. It will be healing to your flesh and strength to your bones."

Proverbs 29:25 "Fearing people is a dangerous trap, but trusting the Lord means safety."

Hebrews 2:13 "He also said, 'I will put my trust in him,' that is, 'I and the children God has given me.'"

Capturing Thoughts: Throughout your adoption journey, I encourage you to capture your thoughts, fears, moments of joy, memories, and challenges. It will be a great encouragement to go back and read what you've written before. Looking back, you'll be surprised how much you and your family grow through your experiences.

Prayer Starter: Lord, it's so easy to doubt myself, especially when people give advice that sounds right. I want to trust you and I do believe that you've called me to this. Give me the strength to lean on you and your word. Give me discernment to know when advice doesn't line up with your purposes and plans for me.

Discussion Questions – Day 8: Double-Minded Instability

1. Can you think of a time that someone gave you well-meaning, but terrible, advice? How did you know not to follow the advice?

2. Today's devotion says, "We cannot allow what someone else thinks or does hold more power over our decisions and family than what God says to do in His Word." Do you struggle with this? If so, talk about how.

3. Read Matthew 16:21-25. This scripture is an example of a time that even Jesus had a well-meaning friend give Him advice that went against the will of the Father. Talk about how Jesus handled the situation and why.

4. Are there decisions or actions that you're being double-minded about? Talk about how you can align with God and move on.

My Journey:

(Use this space to capture your thoughts, prayers, concerns and questions)

LET THE LOWLY BROTHER GLORY IN HIS EXALTATION, BUT THE RICH IN HIS
HUMILIATION, BECAUSE AS A FLOWER OF THE FIELD HE WILL PASS AWAY. FOR NO
SOONER HAS THE SUN RISEN WITH A BURNING HEAT THAN IT WITHERS THE GRASS; ITS
FLOWER FALLS, AND ITS BEAUTIFUL APPEARANCE PERISHES. SO THE RICH MAN ALSO
WILL FADE AWAY IN HIS PURSUITS.

JAMES 1:9-11

DAY 9: IT WILL ALL FADE AWAY

Some of my dearest friends in life are Montell & Kristin Jordan. You
probably know Montell as a 90's R&B star with the mega-hit *This is How We
Do It*. Admit it, you just sang that in your head. I know Montell as a
Worship Pastor at our church and a friend. He and his family are precious
to us. Montell & Kristin have seen the soaring heights of worldly success
and have experienced the devastation of losing it all. After moving to
Atlanta years ago they stood outside their custom built home and watched
as it burned to the ground with all the trappings of wealth, the memories of
their lives, and every worldly possession still inside. I didn't know them
then, but I've seen the video of the devastation and it's horrific to watch.

"One of the first things that I read and understand in today's scripture is that trial and testing have no favorites, they come to everyone."

Knowing them on the other side of their
tragedy, I can tell you that God has truly
brought beautiful things out of the dust of
their lives, literally left in a pile of ash at
their feet. I've watched as God has turned
that tragedy into triumph as they serve Him
without the baggage of things, and with the
wisdom of understanding that if everything

is taken away tomorrow, one thing remains - He is faithful. Their story is a testimony to the truth of this scripture and I've only scratched the surface. I encourage you to look up Montell's book *Becoming Unfamous* and the book he and Kristin wrote together *This Is How We Do It! Making Your Marriage A Masterpeace.*

One of the first things I read and understand in today's scripture is that trial and testing have no favorites, they come to everyone. Your trial might be the current circumstances that you're facing with a difficult child but it could be a lost job, a burned down house, a critical illness, or the death of a loved one. None of us are immune to trial and as we've already established, it's in these times that we trust God and Him alone, counting it all a joy.

As I processed this portion of scripture, the Holy Spirit wouldn't let me settle on this single understanding. I knew what He wanted to communicate wasn't fully developed in my spirit. So I called another dear friend, Allison, who truly has an incredibly deep ability to interpret scripture and communicate understanding. We walked though the text many times, rehearsing God's Word in the context of foster and adoptive families. After settling the words in her heart, Allison said, "Another thing that strikes me about this text is that it's also about refusing to make an idol of our circumstances. We can make a "god" out of anything, even an adoption or foster care process." Wow. Huge confirmation bells rang deep within me.

This concept really applies to any "good" we do in life. We can sometimes get so caught up in the "doing good" that we end up making the work of "doing" our god rather than God and Him only. Right here I want to challenge you and hopefully set you free. I've had adoptive and foster parents say things like, "I'm the only family in our church who has fostered or adopted. If people knew what a mess my family is in, I'm afraid they wouldn't follow God and do it, too."

Let me be perfectly clear. God is absolutely capable of maintaining His own image and it is not up to us to make Him look good in the eyes of other potential foster or adoptive parents. He called us and He can call them. Their obedience is an issue between them and Him, it has nothing to do with you. You don't bear the weight or responsibility of every orphan around the world or every foster child, but you do bear the weight and responsibility of those He has placed in your care.

Every circumstance, every idol, every trial and every opinion will all fade away one day in the light of the presence of our Lord. The gift that's wrapped up for us in this journey is a peace that passes all understanding, regardless of our circumstances, and an ability to make Jesus Christ Lord of our lives and allow everything else to pale in comparison to Him.

Scripture Meditation: Take a few moments to read the following Scriptures. Allow the Holy Spirit to speak to your heart about each of them.

> **Proverbs 11:2** "Pride leads to disgrace, but with humility comes wisdom."

> **Proverbs 16:19** "Better to live humbly with the poor than to share plunder with the proud."

> **Micah 6:8** "No, O people, the Lord has told you what is good, and this is what he requires of you: to do what is right, to love mercy and

walk humbly with your God."

Matthew 6:19-21 "Don't store up treasures here on earth, where moths eat them and rust destroys them, and where thieves break in and steal. Store your treasures in heaven, where moths and rust cannot destroy, and thieves do not break in and steal. Wherever your treasure is, there the desires of your heart will be also. "

Capturing Thoughts: Throughout your adoption journey, I encourage you to capture your thoughts, fears, moments of joy, memories, and challenges. It will be a great encouragement to go back and read what you've written before. Looking back, you'll be surprised how much you and your family grow through your experiences.

Prayer Starter: God, teach us to walk humbly with you. We don't want to make our lives, or anyone in them, an idol that comes before you. Help us as we walk through trials to remember that trial comes to everyone in a multitude of ways.

Discussion Questions – Day 9: It Will All Fade Away

1. In today's devotion, Pam talks about her friend Montell's experience of the height of worldly fame and possessions, losing it all and ultimately discovering purpose in the center of God's will. Is it sometimes hard for you to imagine that other people who seem to "have it all" also experience trials?

2. Read Proverbs 16:19. Do you struggle with pride in wanting your family to be like other families whom you admire? If so, talk about your struggle. Ask God to help you to move away from that kind of comparison.

3. Pam closes today's devotion with this, "Every circumstance, every idol,

every trial and every opinion will all fade away one day in the light of the presence of our Lord. The gift that's wrapped up for us in this journey is a peace that passes all understanding, regardless of our circumstances, and an ability to make Jesus Christ Lord of our lives and allow everything else to pale in comparison to Him." Are there opinions and trials that take precedence over your relationship with the Lord? If so, how can you rearrange those to make God a higher priority?

4. Today's devotion talks about the danger of making our status as foster or adoptive parents an idol in our lives. In what ways does this idea challenge you?

My Journey:

(Use this space to capture your thoughts, prayers, concerns and questions)

BLESSED IS THE MAN WHO ENDURES TEMPTATION; FOR WHEN HE HAS BEEN APPROVED, HE WILL RECEIVE THE CROWN OF LIFE WHICH THE LORD HAS PROMISED TO THOSE WHO LOVE HIM.

JAMES 1:12

DAY 10: ENDURING TEMPTATION

I actually really love today's scripture in the Message version, "Anyone who meets a testing challenge head-on and manages to stick it out is mighty fortunate. For such persons loyally in love with God, the reward is life and more life." The greatest testing challenges that I've ever faced have been in the process of parenting my children and walking with them through the depths of sorrow, grief, loss, and anger at the hand life dealt them. And I find it especially beautiful that here in this verse God calls me fortunate and blessed for having endured them.

Parenting, especially parenting children from hard and difficult places, has been the most refining and humbling experience of my life. An experience requiring literally everything that I had to give - emotionally, physically, and spiritually. Sitting with a child who's experienced profound rejection and trying to find the right words to say, or even pray, is an excruciatingly painful place to sit. Waiting up until all hours of the night on a precious one who may or may not return home is exhausting and challenging. Crying out to God for a peaceful day with a child who is prone to rage-filled outbursts and finding yourself quickly praying again for the strength to respond with grace as you watch the storm brew behind precious eyes full of anger. Feeling the sting of rejection and broken relationship with a precious one who wants nothing to do with the promise of family, and you in particular.

In these moments, and many others, the power of the Cross called me to my knees as I begged for understanding and wisdom, cried out for peace, and mourned the loss of relationship that I had dreamed about and hoped for.

As I've faced the testing challenges of varying trails in being a mom to eight incredible girls - all with hurts, pain and brokenness in their lives, I've failed, and fumbled. I've wanted to give up or give in. And there have been oh so many times that I've sat staring at a new day dawning and wondered if I had the energy to step outside my bedroom door and the grace to keep my words, attitude, and actions right. The truth is that I too have hurts, pain, and brokenness in my life. The shadows of my own childhood cloud my judgment and the pressures of life weigh me down. And, many times, the issues of my heart rise up, and God graciously allows me to see the darkness within me as He leads me to steward my own heart before I even attempt to try to engage with my child(ren). It's a process of continual refining, of God graciously revealing the remnants of darkness that remain in me as a walk with and love my family.

> **"The shadows of my own childhood cloud my judgment and the pressures of life weigh me down."**

Even as I write these words today I find myself struggling with a specific situation in one of my girls who is feeling wounded and hurt by areas where she feels I've failed her as a mom. As I process her hurt, my natural instinct is to defend myself rather than admit the times I've missed an opportunity to be better and more available for her. I want to say, "But don't I have the freedom to have a bad day or a bad couple of years? I've been wading through grief for two solid years. Can you not just give me a little grace?"

67

Yet the Spirit within me isn't going to give me that pass. As one being refined daily into the image of Christ, I have to pastor, teach, and lead my own heart so that I am available to nurture hers. If I enter the discussion with the goal of getting my needs met and making my story important, I will not be able to meet hers and hear her story. Just as she is bringing her hurt and pain to me, her mom, in a vulnerable and courageous way, I must bring my hurt and pain to my Father in heaven and allow Him to nurture my heart and empower me to nurture hers. In this way, I am blessed as I meet the testing-challenge of navigating heart issues, both mine and hers, with the mercy and presence of Jesus surrounding me.

I've come to believe that the role of parent is one of the closest things we will ever experience on this earth resembling the heart of God. And in those moments of deepest heartache, I can imagine God's heart as he longs for a broken, bitter, and angry humanity to turn back to Him and receive the love that He so freely and sacrificially has given. And it is in these moments when we are tempted to lose control and put our needs, hurts, and frustrations before others, that He graciously gives us the strength to endure the temptation and face the challenge with grace and mercy. It is here that we find ourselves experiencing a blessing that only God can provide - a crown of life or as the Message version describes "life and more life."

The gift that is wrapped up for us as we endure temptation and patiently wait on Him to move and bless our circumstances is a transformed heart and mind. A mind that is set on things above and not on the things happening around us. Out of these seasons, He blesses us with life, yet even in that, we have a choice to wake up every day and choose to see the joy before us.

Scripture Meditation: Take a few moments to read the following Scriptures. Allow the Holy Spirit to speak to your heart about each of them.

> **Psalm 138:3** "In the day when I called, You answered me; and You strengthened me with strength (might and inflexibility to temptation) in my inner self."

> **Proverbs 4:14-15** "I will enter not into the path of the wicket, and go not in the way of evil men. I will avoid it, turn from it and pass on."

> **Mark 14:38** "I keep awake and watch and pray (constantly), that I may not enter into temptation, the spirit indeed is willing, but the flesh is weak."

> **Luke 22:40** "I pray to God that I will not be overcome by temptation."

> **James 4:7** "I will be subject to God, I will resist the devil [stand firm against him], and he will flee from me."

Capturing Thoughts: Throughout your adoption journey, I encourage you to capture your thoughts, fears, moments of joy, memories, and challenges. It will be a great encouragement to go back and read what you've written before. Looking back, you'll be surprised how much you and your family grow through your experiences.

Prayer Starter: Jesus, help me to not give into the temptation of self-pity, excuses or denial. Let me boldly accept where I've done wrong and repent to you, and to my family. Help me to also avoid the temptation to doubt, gossip, or be lazy as I seek to do your will in my family. Thank you that you will never leave me or forsake me and even when I don't see a way out, I can trust you to guide me.

Discussion Questions – Day 10: Enduring Temptation

1. Think about a time that you have been tempted. Explain how you overcame or gave in to the temptation. What was the result of your choice?

2. Temptation often arises most when we are exhausted or emotionally drained. What are some boundaries that you need in your life to help you in these moments?

3. In today's devotion Pam talks about her own childhood and emotions getting in the way as she's trying to follow God and parent her children. Do you ever find yourself struggling with something related to your own childhood? If so, how can you get some extra support in that area?

4. Today's devotion talks about the role of a parent being a living example of God's heart. How has parenting helped you to better understand the heart of God?

My Journey:

(Use this space to capture your thoughts, prayers, concerns and questions)

BLESSED IS THE MAN WHO ENDURES TEMPTATION; FOR WHEN HE HAS BEEN APPROVED,
HE WILL RECEIVE THE CROWN OF LIFE WHICH THE LORD HAS PROMISED TO THOSE
WHO LOVE HIM.

JAMES 1:12

DAY 11: THE CROWN OF LIFE

I'm writing this as we round the corner into another brand new year. For the past couple of years I've participated in the "one word" challenge to choose a word that I will focus on for the year. This year I chose the word LIFE because Jesus promised in John 10:10 that He had come so that we could have life and have it more abundantly. In choosing this word, I committed in my heart to experience the fullness of life in Him every day of the year. The reason that I feel like the Holy Spirit led me to that scripture and word is because I desperately needed to set my mind on the joy and fulfillment that God through Jesus has for me right here, right now in every moment.

There is no better way to describe the experience of the past few years than as a crucible of suffering. Many of my girls were experiencing the lowest of lows in their lives as they emerged from being teenagers into the scary independence of adulthood, while others were experiencing the highest of highs, three of them marrying the love of their lives in the past two years. In the middle of it, all friends and family that I dearly loved exchanged their earthly addresses for heavenly ones. It felt like I could barely catch a breath before the phone rang again. I wore the same black dress to so many funerals that I finally threw it in the trash because I couldn't stand to look at it again. To say that I desperately needed a fresh outlook and a new

72

perspective was an understatement.

Through it all I've never lost sight of who God is in my life, but my heart was certainly heavily burdened. As I endured the testing challenges of the past couple of years, there was always a temptation to wallow in self-pity, or to give up fighting in the areas that God had given me responsibility over— my family, my marriage, and the nonprofit that He called me to start. It was an intentional and conscious effort to refuse to allow the enemy to steal those things even when my heart was breaking in grief and exhaustion. It's here, in this type of endurance, in meeting the testing challenges head on, that God blesses us and He gives us the crown of life.

> **"There is certainly a crown of life awaiting us in heaven as we stand before our King and receive His honor for the life we've lived to glorify Him."**

There is certainly a crown of life awaiting us in heaven as we stand before our King and receive His honor for the life we've lived to glorify Him. There is also a crown of life that we can experience right here, right now in the midst of our suffering and trials, what Paul in Philippians 4:7 calls, "the peace that passes all understanding which guards our hearts and minds in Christ Jesus." That ability, found only in Christ, that allows us to stand in the winner's circle of life with the tempest of winds blowing around us as we calmly and joyfully practice endurance, patience, and our perfect faith in Him, and Him alone.

The gift we're unwrapping as we boldly face the testing challenges that come upon us is the opportunity to grow our faith and learn how to choose life and more life even as we walk through the valley of the shadow grief,

heartbreak, and even death

Scripture Meditation: Take a few moments to read the following Scriptures. Allow the Holy Spirit to speak to your heart about each of them.

> **Job 22:21** "Now yield and submit yourself to Him [agree with God and be conformed to His will] and be at peace; in this way [you will prosper and great] good will come to you."

> **Isaiah 26:3** "You will keep in perfect and constant peace the one whose mind is steadfast [that is, committed and focused on You—in both inclination and character], because he trusts and takes refuge in You [with hope and confident expectation]."

> **John 14:27** "Peace I leave with you; my [perfect] peace I give to you; not as the world gives do I give to you. Do not let your heart be troubled, nor let it be afraid. [Let My perfect peace calm you in every circumstance and give you courage and strength for every challenge.]"

> **2 Thessalonians 3:16** "Now may the Lord of peace Himself grant you His peace at all times and in every way [that peace and spiritual well-being that comes to those who walk with Him, regardless of life's circumstances]. The Lord be with you all."

Capturing Thoughts: Throughout your adoption journey, I encourage you to capture your thoughts, fears, moments of joy, memories, and challenges. It will be a great encouragement to go back and read what you've written before. Looking back, you'll be surprised how much you and your family grow through your experiences.

Prayer Starter: Jesus, thank you for giving us the strength to endure every trial that this life might throw our way. We know that perfect peace is found in you and in you alone. We commit to hiding ourselves in your word so that our foundation cannot be shaken, regardless of our circumstance.

Discussion Questions – Day 11: The Crown of Life

1. Have you ever thought about what it means to have the peace that passes all understanding? You don't need that kind of peace when things are going well; you need it when life is throwing its worst at you. Talk about a time you've experienced that type of peace in the midst of difficulty.

2. In today's devotion Pam shares what she calls the "crucible of suffering" in her own life. what does that mean to you?

3. Do you struggle with letting your emotions rule you during trials? Are there practical things that you can change to make it easier?

4. As you think about your own measure of peace in trials, how can you transfer this understanding to your children whose lives have been full of suffering? Have you ever considered your own peace journey as a living testimony of God's grace for your children? Talk about how this idea challenges or excites you.

My Journey:

(Use this space to capture your thoughts, prayers, concerns and questions)

LET NO ONE SAY WHEN HE IS TEMPTED, "I AM TEMPTED BY GOD"; FOR GOD CANNOT

BE TEMPTED BY EVIL, NOR DOES HE HIMSELF TEMPT ANYONE.

JAMES 1:13

DAY 12: AN UNVEILED HEART

I'm an absolute sucker for cute YouTube videos of cats or kids, much to my husband's dismay as I make him watch them fully believing that he should get the same level of pleasure and joy from them as I do. The other day I watched an utterly cute video of a little girl who had painted her Barbie doll's finger nails with real fingernail polish on the carpet of her bedroom. Through adorable little tears she tries to convince her dad that Barbie asked her to paint them, even when she told Barbie that she couldn't do it, Barbie insisted. It's a four-year old's version of "the devil made me do it." Haven't we all been there?

Far too often in my own walk with the Lord, I've found myself trying to convince myself and even God that my sin was a result of the trial that He put into my life that caused me to stumble. It's my own personal version of Adam's response to God, "...that woman you gave me made me do it." But just like the dad in that YouTube video knew that Barbie had nothing to do with his sweet daughter following through on her desire to use nail polish in her room when she knew it was wrong, God knew that Eve, though present and guilty, didn't *make* Adam eat the fruit of the tree. Just like He knows that my sin is mine, and He isn't to blame - nor did He cause it.

As we face the trials, challenges and frustrations of life and family there will always be a gazillion and one ways that the enemy can tempt us into sin by presenting us with doubt, anger, bitterness, resentment, and the list goes on. When we're frustrated at something that our kids are doing, do we work it out with God in prayer or do we rehearse it with our friends on the phone—giving our frustrations voice and a chance to take root within us as resentment? It's never too hard to find one or five friends who will agree with your feelings, sign off on your

> "It's never too hard to find one or five friends who will agree with your feelings, sign off on your actions and validate your 'rights.' The question isn't were you justified, the question should always be is it Christ-like?"

actions and validate your "rights." The question isn't were you justified, the question should always be *is it Christ-like?* I've even watched this play out in my marriage from time to time when either Steve or I are upset by something one of our kids has done and we give "our version" of events to one another tainted by our emotions and ultimately sowing a seed of strife into our hearts and family. Inevitably the other spouse, if we aren't extremely careful, takes on the viewpoint of storyteller and aligns in agreement with whatever feelings and actions are being discussed. At times this type of discussion can be used and manipulated by the enemy of our souls as he seeks to use our oneness against us by aligning us to bitterness, resentment, anger, and self-pity. Tread carefully. Being aligned with your spouse in every area of life is a true gift of God in marriage, and as is typical of the enemy, he attacks and tempts us right in the midst of a good gift of God to get us off course and ultimately, into sin.

We must always remember that God is not the author of sin or the temptation to sin—ever. We've already established that difficulties come into our lives for our good, and even when they are placed in our lives by God, they are designed to help us grow. His design is for the fruits of grace, mercy, and perseverance to be the result as we are molded into His image. The enemy of our souls has a different agenda all together. He will come in as a thought or feeling of frustration, or will take an opportunity during a point of exhaustion to have a friend say something that tempts us into moving away from God's designed result and into our self-protective emotions and feelings.

Temptation is never authored by God, but sometimes the fiery trial that He is allowing us to endure exposes areas where we are vulnerable to it. As I've faced the testing challenges of my life, they have often revealed the selfishness of my heart and the darkness that hides there, which is so easily masked when things are going my way. The gift that's wrapped up for us in the fiery trial is the ability to recognize the deceiver and tempter in our midst as we walk through the fire that unveils the darkness of our heart; learning to trust the still, small voice of the Lord over the loud clanging of our emotions, selfish desires, and fleeting feelings.

Scripture Meditation: Take a few moments to read the following Scriptures. Allow the Holy Spirit to speak to your heart about each of them.

> **Psalm 46:1** "God is my refuge and strength [mighty and impenetrable to temptation], a very present and well-proved help in trouble."

> **Psalm 138:3** "In the day when I called, You answered me; and You strengthened me with strength (might and inflexibility to temptation)

in my inner self."

Mark 14:38 "I keep awake and watch and pray [constantly], that I may not enter into temptation; the spirit indeed is willing, the flesh is weak."

Luke 22:40 "I pray to God that I will not be overcome by temptation."

Romans 12:21 "I will not let myself be overcome with evil, but will overcome (master) evil with good."

1 Corinthians 10:13 MSG "No test or temptation that comes your way is beyond the course of what others have had to face. All you need to remember is that God will never let you down; he'll never let you be pushed past your limit; he'll always be there to help you come through it."

Capturing Thoughts: Throughout your adoption journey, I encourage you to capture your thoughts, fears, moments of joy, memories, and challenges. It will be a great encouragement to go back and read what you've written before. Looking back, you'll be surprised how much you and your family grow through your experiences.

Prayer Starter: Father, thank you that you are present with me, always. Help me to avoid the temptations of the enemy whether they come in the quiet of my own heart, through the well-meaning words of a friend, or from my own desire for restored peace in my home. Give me the strength, wisdom and understanding to discern the evil from the good and to look to you, the author and the finisher of my faith and my family.

Discussion Questions – Day 12: An Unveiled Heart

1. What's your biggest obstacle when it comes to carving out time to diligently read the Word? Talk about ways you can overcome that obstacle.

2. Read Psalm 46:1. What role does diligent Bible reading play in the Lord being a refuge and strength in times of trouble?

3. Today's devotion talks about the temptation. From the beginning of time, Satan has been tempting us to sin. Although he may present us with an opinion, thought or idea that sounds reasonable, we must always apply the Word of the Lord to it, and stop and ask God. He will always faithfully direct and guide us. Write down some recent thoughts, ideas or opinions that you need to filter through with the Lord before taking actions, or making decisions.

4. Write down two promises from God's Word for your family. Mediate on those throughout the day. Make note of how your faith increases as you put this simple practice into place.

My Journey:

(Use this space to capture your thoughts, prayers, concerns and questions)

DAY 13: ENTICED BY OUR OWN DESIRES

It is in our sinful and unredeemed nature to desire. Greed, selfishness, pride, and lust are baked into us at birth due to the broken world we're born into and our innate need for a Savior to rescue and redeem us. In adoption and foster care circles, we often get into conversations about how sad it is that more people won't open their homes to children in desperate need of families, or that more churches won't challenge their congregations to step up in the face of such overwhelming need. It's a legitimate problem, but if we aren't careful behind our "holy discontent" can be a silent judgment on people who choose not to enter foster care and adoption. Let's be honest, sometimes we feel and think that they're greedy and selfish—protecting their "perfect little family" rather than stepping out in faith and trusting God. We think it's selfish and prideful. We assume that their lust for comfort and ease are greater than their desire to do a good work for God.

Inwardly you were nodding your head as you read that last paragraph, probably thinking, "Yeah, I've had those kind of thoughts before. I'll do better about not being judgmental.... but still...." Careful. Our pride is showing. I hope you chuckled at this because we're all guilty. Even as I typed this, I am guilty. It's always easier to point out the desires and sin in others than it is to look at it within ourselves. Yet, it's there. It's in me, and in you. Even in the very center of the good work that we're doing in our families and communities, we have desires that can entice us into sin.

We're all familiar with the story of David and Bathsheba. David, King over all of Israel, is minding his own business on the roof and when he looks across and sees a beautiful woman bathing, immediately his natural desires and lust are awakened. Her beauty entices him and he can't get her out of his mind. At this point in the story, David has done nothing sinful (with Bathsheba at least—the fact that he's not at war is another story). He isn't aware that she's married and he is simply a man who has accidentally viewed a beautiful woman; albeit naked and bathing, but that's not the point. David is tempted and he is being enticed by his own desires. Here in the story he still has the opportunity to do the right and righteous thing— walk away and run the kingdom that God has entrusted him with which, by the way, is at war. David the king should be on the battlefield with his men, not on the roof where temptation has a chance to entice him.

David's story is our story, too, we just don't realize it. We're simply trying to do the right thing in the story that God has called us into and suddenly we're sidelined by our own heart's tendency toward selfishness, greed, pride or lust. And one of the greatest desires that I see entice foster and adoptive families, and even my own heart, is the desire for "everything to just go back to normal." Before the trauma, before the lying, before the rages, before the disconnected relationship, before the suffering in our marriage, before..... everything. Here in our story we still

> **"We're simply trying to do the right thing in the story that God has called us into and suddenly we're sidelined by our own heart's tendency toward selfishness, greed, pride and lust."**

have the opportunity to do the right and righteous thing—walk away and participate in the family that God has entrusted us to, which by the way, is at war - a deep spiritual one for our hearts and minds. We, as the guardians of our homes, should be on the battlefield in prayer and not focused on our fickle and fleeting emotions and feelings which tempt and entice us.

It's easy for us to see this pattern in the lives of others, yet God is calling us higher and asking us to guard and steward our own hearts by recognizing the greed that tells us that we must protect what we have at all costs, the selfishness that focuses on what we want and need rather than needs of others, the pride of self righteousness, and the lust for comfort and ease that draws us away from the deep and challenging things that make us more like Him.

The gift that God is so graciously allowing us to unwrap is a laying aside of our own desires so that His work can be made complete within us and our lives can shine as a reflection of His goodness and glory.

Scripture Meditation: Take a few moments to read the following Scriptures. Allow the Holy Spirit to speak to your heart about each of them.

> **Mark 8:34** "I am not selfish and self-centered. I deny myself, I take up my cross and follow Jesus. I forget myself, lose sight of myself and all my own interests."

> **Philippians 2:3-7** "I do nothing out of selfish ambition or vain conceit, but in humility consider others better than myself. I look not only to my own interests, but also to the interests of others. My

attitude is the same as that of Christ Jesus: Who, being in the very nature God, did not consider equality with God something to be grasped, but made Himself nothing."

1 Timothy 5:6 "I don't live just for pleasure and self-gratification [giving myself up to luxury and self-indulgence] for the one who does this is dead even while they still live."

1 John 3:17-18 "But whoever has this world's goods, and sees his brother in need, and shuts up his heart from him, how does the love of God abide in him? I do not love in word or in tongue, but in deed and in truth."

Capturing Thoughts: Throughout your adoption journey, I encourage you to capture your thoughts, fears, moments of joy, memories, and challenges. It will be a great encouragement to go back and read what you've written before. Looking back, you'll be surprised how much you and your family grow through your experiences.

Prayer Starter: Father, help us to set aside our own desires, which lead us into temptation. We understand that temptation doesn't come from you, but from the enemy of our souls. We also understand that our own desires can often open the door for temptation to enter our hearts and for us to act on it. Help us to develop a strong heart to know you, and only you, so that the desires of our hearts and the words of our mouths reflect you.

Discussion Questions – Day 13: Enticed by Our Own Desires

1. Talk about a time that you had a strong desire for something that you knew wasn't necessarily the most wise thing. How did you feel after your desire was achieved?

2. Philippians 2:3-7. God knows the ambitions of the human heart and how difficult it is to put the needs of others above our own desires. Jesus understood this so well that He willingly kept himself on the Cross on our behalf. Take a moment to examine your heart. Are there needs that your children and family have that you're putting aside because of your own desires or ambitions?

3. In today's devotion, Pam talks about the "desire for normal" being a big temptation that often leads foster and adoptive families astray. Has that desire been an issue for you? What are three practical things you can do to protect your heart when it's vulnerable and tired?

4. What's one need in your family that's fallen out of focus you can immediately put back on the priority list?

My Journey:

(Use this space to capture your thoughts, prayers, concerns and questions)

THEN, WHEN DESIRE HAS CONCEIVED, IT GIVES BIRTH TO SIN; AND SIN, WHEN IT IS

FULL-GROWN, BRINGS FORTH DEATH.

JAMES 1:15

DAY 14: DESIRE BECOMES SIN

Yesterday we looked at the story of David and Bathsheba and how in an unplanned and unexpected moment David caught sight of her and his desire was awakened. The trouble for David began when *in his heart* he determined to make her his. So he inquired about her, learned that she was Uriah's wife, sent for her anyway, slept with her, and she conceived a child. David's desire became sin the moment that his heart made up its mind about a course of action as a result of the temptation that was in front of him.

In the same way, there are things that can tempt us or that we desire in our innate human nature. Like David, we don't have to act on those temptations or desires, we have a choice. In order to protect ourselves, we have to be extremely careful of those things that we "determine in our heart." Sin isn't conceived simply because we have a thought or even a desire. The enemy can tempt us into thinking and wanting anything at any given moment. The problem happens when we come into agreement with those thoughts in our heart and begin to entertain the thoughts and form them into ideas and action.

In my life, there have been plenty of times, especially as a parent, that I've allowed my desire to cloud my judgment and tempt me. Sometimes it's something as simple as the desire for everything to "go back to normal"

89

that can lead us to fantasizing about what life would be like without all of the current stress and trauma. Our fantasy turns to sin as we rehearse it with others and find ourselves actively looking for ways to escape—emotionally and physically. If we're not careful, an innocent desire can begin to transform into a root of bitterness, anger, resentment, and turn into a deep-seeded malice toward our situation and everyone involved. Soon we find ourselves distant and checked-out, becoming hard-hearted to the work that the Lord is trying to do in our midst and possibly even hindering it.

> **"If we're not careful, an innocent desire can begin to transform into a root of bitterness, anger and resentment and turn into a deep-seeded malice toward our situation, and everyone involved."**

None of us start here. We don't ever say, "I want to foster or adopt a child who is broken and alone and then I want to get angry and frustrated and end up resenting that child." Even writing that seems ridiculous, yet that's exactly where the enemy can lead us if we're not mindful of our desires and how easy it is for those desires to lead us into actions that betray our faith and our Christ-like intentions.

As we move onward in our refining as sons and daughters being molded daily into the image of our Heavenly Father, it is a great gift to develop the strength to withstand the wiles of the enemy and become sensitive to the Holy Spirit as He gently leads us away from temptation and into the glorious promises of God, which are salvation to us and our families.

Scripture Meditation: Take a few moments to read the following Scriptures. Allow the Holy Spirit to speak to your heart about each of them.

> **Psalm 1:1** "I am blessed, happy, fortunate, prosperous, and to be envied because I walk and live not in the counsel of the ungodly [following their advice, their plans and purposes], nor do I stand [submissive and inactive] in the path where sinners walk, nor sit down [to relax and rest] where the scornful [and the mockers] gather."

> **Psalm 119:2-3** "I search for God and always do His will, rejecting compromise with evil and walking only in His paths."

> **Hebrews 11:25** "I prefer to suffer the hardships of the people of God rather than to have the fleeting enjoyment of a sinful life."

> **2 Timothy 2:22** "Run from anything that stimulates youthful lusts. Instead pursue righteous living, faithfulness, love and peace. Enjoy the companionship of those who call on the Lord with pure hearts."

Capturing Thoughts: Throughout your adoption journey, I encourage you to capture your thoughts, fears, moments of joy, memories, and challenges. It will be a great encouragement to go back and read what you've written before. Looking back, you'll be surprised how much you and your family grow through your experiences.

Prayer Starter: Lord, thank you for giving us your Word as a guide and showing us, through David, how easily we can fall into the trap of desire, temptation, and sin. Give us strength to walk in your ways: in faithfulness, love, purity, peace, and kindness. Help us to lay aside our sinful desires and selfish lusts for comfort so that we can faithfully accomplish the work you have set before us.

Discussion Questions – Day 14: Desire Becomes Sin

1. Describe a time that you allowed desire to become sin in your life. What were the consequences? How did you overcome?

2. Think back to when you began your journey into foster care or adoption. If someone had given you a mirror into the future and you had seen the difficulty that lay ahead, would you have continued? What about this journey has made it worth it?

3. In today's devotion, Pam talks about our innocent desire for peace leading to fantasy about a life we wish we could live. In the end, she says that this could lead us to being distant and checked out. Does this description resonate with you? Talk about how you're feeling.

4. Why is it important for you to be continually mindful of your desires?

My Journey:

(Use this space to capture your thoughts, prayers, concerns and questions)

THEN, WHEN DESIRE HAS CONCEIVED, IT GIVES BIRTH TO SIN; AND SIN, WHEN IT IS
FULL-GROWN, BRINGS FORTH DEATH.

JAMES 1:15

DAY 15: SIN KILLS

As we continue forward in the story of David and Bathsheba, we find
David needing to cover his sin—the now pregnant Bathsheba. He sends
word to have her husband sent to the front lines of battle knowing that it's
a guarantee of certain death. Uriah's death freed David to marry Bathsheba
(in an attempt to cover his sin of adultery). As a result, their first born son
dies as the Lord deals with David and confronts him on his sin and betrayal
of Uriah. Desire gave birth to sin and sin brought forth literal death, twice.

Sin literally kills the promises and possibilities that God has for our families
and for us. We may not experience actual death, but we do experience the
death of purpose because we allowed the enemy to sideline and derail us.
All it takes is a quick look around us to see the result of sin on our world
and in our families. Divorce rips apart even Christian families. Kids who are
caught in the middle sometimes struggle well into adulthood to come to
grips with the pain they suffered when the safe, secure world of their family
fell apart. As foster and adoptive families, we regularly deal with the result
of sin when we parent children whose lives were ripped apart by drug
addiction, teenage sex, sex outside of marriage, a country of origin bound in
the depths of poverty by corrupt government leaders, and much more.

We cannot risk our families and God's promises on the altar of desire. Our
culture has convinced us that we are entitled to indulgence and convenience

in every area of life. Earthly culture has always been in sharp contrast to Kingdom culture and if we measure our success and failures by the world's standards rather than God's standards, we will fall woefully short of obtaining the gift he has set aside for us in this life. Death of our God-sized dreams and God-given purpose can only come if we give temptation and sin a foothold.

> **"We cannot risk our families and God's promises on the altar of desire."**

Earthly culture tells us we are bad parents if our children rebel, backtalk, or misbehave. Kingdom culture tells us that sin is innate in each of us and we are to love others (this includes our children) as we've been loved. We have rebelled, we have back-talked, and we have misbehaved and our Heavenly Father has never forsaken His love for us or desired to cast us out. Earthly culture tells us that we should control every outcome of our children's lives. Kingdom culture tells us that we are to train them according to their gifting and the Word. God loves them more than we ever could, even in our best moments.

Sin and temptations easily take over in our hearts, minds, attitudes, and actions. It's only as we walk closely in relationship with our Lord, and one another that we can maintain a purity of heart and purpose that keep us free from sin, free from earthly desires, and free to love ourselves and our children with grace and understanding. Quite simply, a heart that is protected from temptation and sin by humbly surrendering to Jesus is a heart that understands the greatest gift of all, God's abounding grace.

Scripture Meditation: Take a few moments to read the following Scriptures. Allow the Holy Spirit to speak to your heart about each of them.

> **Psalm 37:7** "Be still in the presence of the Lord, and wait patiently for him to act. Don't worry about evil people who prosper or fret about their wicked schemes."

> **Psalm 39:7-8** "And so, Lord, where do I put my hope? My only hope is in you. Rescue me from my rebellion. Do not let fools mock me."

> **Psalm 62:1-2** "I wait quietly before God, for my victory comes from him. He alone is my rock and my salvation, my fortress where I will never be shaken."

> **Habakkuk 2:3** "This vision is for a future time. It describes the end, and it will be fulfilled. If it seems slow in coming, wait patiently, for it will surely take place. It will not be delayed."

Capturing Thoughts: Throughout your adoption journey, I encourage you to capture your thoughts, fears, moments of joy, memories, and challenges. It will be a great encouragement to go back and read what you've written before. Looking back, you'll be surprised how much you and your family grow through your experiences.

Prayer Starter: Lord, thank you for protecting me from sin through your Word. Give me the ability to wait patiently, to endure the trial, to trust that your promises are true and will come to pass, even if I feel like it's taking too long. Help me, Lord, to not take matters into my own hands. You are God and you don't need my help. In trusting you, I am confident that the dreams you've given me for my family will come to pass and will not die.

Discussion Questions – Day 15: Sin Kills

1. Do you feel like culture's version of a "normal" or "perfect" family ever drives you to present a false version? Or cause you to resent the gift of your family "as is," warts and all?

2. Today's devotion says, "We cannot risk our families and God's promises on the altar of desire." Have you ever considered the negative consequences to "giving up" and having family "your way"? What do you think some negative outcomes could be?

3. Read Habakkuk 2:3. How difficult is it for you to imagine that the vision you have for your family might be slow in coming? Can you trust the Lord that it will ultimately come to pass?

4. What are some of the fears you keep hidden because you worry about what others will think? How can this group pray for you in these areas?

My Journey:

(Use this space to capture your thoughts, prayers, concerns and questions)

DAY 16: DO NOT BE DECEIVED

Deception is everywhere. Spend five minutes on Facebook and you're inundated with news stories from less than credible sources designed to provoke fear, anger, division, and confusion. These "fake news" articles are often dumped into our newsfeeds by large tabloid-type organizations geared to get as many clicks, likes, shares, and comments as possible in order to drive their reach and, ultimately, increase their ad revenues. The bottom line motivators for this insidious practice that sometimes deceives even the most careful observer are money, power, and control.

Fake news on social media is a great analogy for how the enemy of our souls seeks to deceive us on a daily basis. Every single day, unseen by our naked eye, billions of spiritual beings circulate "fake news" into our hearts, minds, emotions, and environments in order to provoke fear, anger, division, and confusion. The motivators are the same: power and control; the ultimate profit (for them) or loss (to us), however, is much worse—this enemy seeks our very souls. He's clever enough to know that if he can't get us to completely turn away from God, the next best thing is to get us caught up in our emotions, feelings, and frustrations as we blame God and one another for the things happening around us.

We must be vigilant to guard our hearts and minds against the deceiver. This is especially true when we are exhausted, emotionally raw, and spiritually starved because the demands of a difficult or challenging season with a child, or many, have left us battle-weary and battle-worn. These moments are when we are at our most vulnerable, and that's exactly when the enemy will strike with accusations like, "You're not doing enough," doubts like, "Did we make the right decision?" and fears like, "This is never going to get better." This is fake news! Be careful to not come into agreement with these lie or to share them as truth. Take them to the filter of our Father and let the Holy Spirit speak truth as you cast the deceiver aside and point your vulnerable soul in the direction of Jesus.

I love the gentle way James closes the statement with, "my beloved brethren." It's a sweet reminder that we're all in this together and although our stories may look different, our enemy and our Redeemer are the same. Look around today for a safe place with two or three trusted and Christ-centered friends. Pour your fears, failures, and frustrations out in prayer among these fellow believers who will take your hand and

"Do not be deceived, precious ones, our enemy the devil is roaming around looking for those whom he might devour. His sole goal is to steal, kill, and destroy the gift of God within you."

walk into God's presence alongside you. Do not be deceived, precious ones, our enemy the devil is roaming around looking for those whom he might devour. His sole goal is to steal, kill, and destroy the gift of God within you.

Scripture Meditation: Take a few moments to read the following Scriptures. Allow the Holy Spirit to speak to your heart about each of them.

Galatians 6:6-8 "Do not be deceived: God is not mocked, for whatever one sows, that will he also reap. For the one who sows to his own flesh will from the flesh reap corruption, but the one who sows to the Spirit will from the Spirit reap eternal life."

Revelation 12:9 "And the great dragon was thrown down, the serpent of old who is called the devil and Satan, who deceives the whole world; he was thrown down to earth, and his angels were thrown down with him."

1 John 4:1 "Beloved, do not believe every spirit, but test the spirits to see whether they are from God, because many false prophets have gone out into the world."

2 Corinthians 11:3 "But I am afraid that, as the serpent deceived Eve by his craftiness, your minds will be led astray from the simplicity and purity of devotion to Christ."

2 Corinthians 11:13-15 "For such men are false apostles, deceitful workers, disguising themselves as apostles of Christ. No wonder, for even Satan disguises himself as an angel of light. Therefore it is not surprising if his servants also disguise themselves as servants of righteousness, whose end will be according to their deeds."

Capturing Thoughts: Throughout your adoption journey, I encourage you to capture your thoughts, fears, moments of joy, memories, and challenges. It will be a great encouragement to go back and read what you've written before. Looking back, you'll be surprised how much you and your family grow through your experiences.

Prayer Starter: Father, help us to not be led into deception by the enemy's "fake news." Give us the ability to trust in you so that we aren't mislead. We know that many times the enemy's schemes seem right and they may even feel right, but help us to filter them through the truth of the word and remove any blinders from our eyes so that we may see and know you, and only you.

Discussion Questions – Day 16: Do Not Be Deceived

1. Read 2 Corinthians 11:13-15. In what ways does Satan disguise himself as a angel of light?

2. Today's devotion says, "We must be vigilant to guard our hearts and minds against the deceiver. This is especially true when we are exhausted, emotionally raw and spiritually starved because the demands of a difficult or challenging season with a child, or many, have left us battle-weary and battle-worn." Describe a time that you've felt emotionally raw or spiritually starved because of the demands of a difficult season. How did you find help to restore your strength? If you're in that season now, how can you find help?

3. Pam describes the enemy's lies as "fake news." Make a list of "fake news" that the enemy is trying to get you to believe and align with even now.

4. Discuss any emotions that you're struggling with that might be making it hard to discern God's will. How can this group pray for you and with you?

My Journey:

(Use this space to capture your thoughts, prayers, concerns and questions)

DAY 17: OUR GOOD & PERFECT GIFT

Today's scripture is the central point of this entire devotional—*the gift* of God is good and perfect. I love this verse, and I love the truthfulness of this picture of our Heavenly Father. He is the Father of lights, our good God in whom dwells no ill intention, no sin, and no desire for anything but our good. In Him there is no variation or shadow of turning. He is the same today as He was from the beginning. He will be the same tomorrow as He is today. God, unlike you and me, never changes and, also unlike you and me, never has anything but the absolute best intentions for us, His beloved children.

I vividly remember when Steve and I started our journey into foster care and adoption. We were excited and nervous, expecting the best things from this wonderful gift of adoption that would grow our family. We dutifully attended class, completed our mountain of paperwork and prepared our daughter for the addition of a sister. Sheer elation marked our every action and thought. We could not wait for the day we were able to meet our daughter. We absolutely viewed the addition of this precious child as a gift to our family, and we prayed we would be a gift to her. Imagine our surprise when we arrived on the day that we were to meet her for the very first time and her case manager met us in the parking lot of the group home she lived in with the warning, "Don't be surprised if she's not happy that

104

you're here." This warning was followed by seeing this precious little girl that we'd dreamed of meeting get off of the school bus and purposely walk right past us without even a glance. She truly didn't want us there. "The gift" we were unwrapping certainly wasn't what we had expected.

> **"There were many times that our "gift" of growing our family through foster care and adoption seemed far from good, and certainly far from perfect. Yet, even so, it was."**

Eleven years later, that spunky and spirited little girl is a precious 22-year-old that we proudly call daughter, and she proudly calls us Dad and Mom. A good and perfect gift, indeed. Yet, it didn't always look that way. There have been many moments along this eleven year journey full of bitterness, anger, rejection, betrayal, selfishness, rebellion, rage, and more—from all of us. There were many times that our "gift" of growing our family through foster care and adoption seemed far from good, and certainly far from perfect. Yet, even so, it was.

I heard a story once about a Christian farmer who faithfully planted a crop. Not long after he had planted the crop he noticed that the seed in his field wasn't sprouting above the surface, but all of his neighbors' seeds were. He asked God, "Why have you given me a failed crop? Now my family will go hungry." Three days later a major wind and hail storm came and it destroyed all of the crops. A few days after the storm passed, his field began to sprout. Because his crop had been slower to sprout, it had been spared the battering of the wind and it flourished. The same farmer was getting old and frail and only had one son to help him with the harvest. One day his son was working in the field and he fell and broke his leg. He asked God, "Why have you allowed my son to break his leg, now it will be twice as difficult to bring in the harvest?" A few days later, a group of rebel soldiers came by his farm looking for able-bodied young men to force into their ranks, but upon seeing his son's condition they passed by and left him. A delayed harvest and broken bones are certainly not something that any of us would consider good gifts. However, God, in His infinite mercy, allowed those things because He knew what the farmer didn't, that even the hardships can be a gift used for our good, and they are perfect.

In our family the gift of foster care and adoption didn't look like what we expected it to look like. It wasn't as easy as we thought it would be. It was painful, scary, and often times exhausting. Even so, it was a good and perfect gift from our heavenly father who in His infinite wisdom brought grace, mercy, love, humility, sacrifice, kindness and light into our family in ways that only He could do. He is a good, good father.

Scripture Meditation: Take a few moments to read the following Scriptures. Allow the Holy Spirit to speak to your heart about each of them.

> **Psalm 34:8** "Oh taste and see that the Lord [our God] is good! Blessed (happy, fortunate, to be envied) is the man who trusts and takes refuge in Him."

> **Psalm 84:11** "The Lord God is my Sun and Shield; the Lord bestows [present] grace and favor and [future] glory (honor, splendor, and heavenly bliss)! No good thing will He withhold from me as I walk uprightly."

> **Jeremiah 29:11** "For I know the plans I have for you, says the Lord, plans to prosper you and not to harm you, plans to give you a hope and a future."

Jeremiah 33:11 "The Lord is good; for His mercy, tender kindness and steadfast love endure forever."

Capturing Thoughts: Throughout your adoption journey, I encourage you to capture your thoughts, fears, moments of joy, memories, and challenges. It will be a great encouragement to go back and read what you've written before. Looking back, you'll be surprised how much you and your family grow through your experiences.

Prayer Starter: Lord, thank you for your goodness. Thank you that you give good and perfect gifts to me, even though I don't always recognize them in the moment. Today, I just want to bring honor to you in my prayer and praise because you are so good and your love is patient, kind, tender, and lasts forever. Thank you for the great kindness you've shown me. And, thank you for the gift of your Son Jesus and His obedience to the Cross that gave me the best gift of all, knowing you as my Father and Him as my Savior and King for eternity.

Discussion Questions – Day 17: Our Good & Perfect Gift

1. Have you ever gotten a gift that at first you didn't like, but later realized just how much you needed it? Talk about that gift and how that relates to the way that God's gifts show up in our lives.

2. In today's devotion, Pam tells the story of a farmer and his son. Can you relate to this story in your own life? Talk about a time that something seemingly bad turned into something good.

3. Do you struggle to see the good in your family's story when things are going poorly? Is there something you can do to remind yourself of truth during difficulty?

4. Choose a scripture from today's devotion to stand upon as a family. Share the scripture you chose with your group and why you chose it.

My Journey:

(Use this space to capture your thoughts, prayers, concerns and questions)

OF HIS OWN WILL HE BROUGHT US FORTH BY THE WORD OF TRUTH, THAT WE MIGHT

BE A KIND OF FIRST-FRUITS OF HIS CREATURES.

JAMES 1:18

DAY 18: BORN OF TRUTH

We've watched three of our daughters walk down the aisle to meet the love of their lives at beautifully adorned altars. Weddings—they are beautiful days full of happiness and joy. Every single wedding was proceeded by months of planning, perfecting, and practicing for the "big day." As I watched our daughters walk down the aisle on their Daddy's arm, I was filled with a love and pride that is indescribable. This moment was a result of many years of prayer over our precious girls, and many months of planning to make it beautiful and perfect. Each wedding was a brilliant and public display of love for our daughter, and her love for her husband. Each one brought forth because we loved our girls and they were ours. When I read today's scripture, I remember those moments and many others where I stood in pride as my children received an award, accomplished a goal, or displayed character and integrity that reflected the dreams we had for them because they are ours.

Each of our girls is a part of our family because we either physically brought them into the world or chose them to be a part of our family. They are the first fruits of our family, the reflection of our family that gets presented to the world. We, of course, want it to be a good reflection. We stand in pride at those moments because those moments are the pay off for our sacrifices, and the result of our family values and climate, in every good and bad way possible. If we stop for a moment and consider all of the ways we work to present our children to the world as reflections of us—from toothpaste bows on tiny bald newborn heads, to perfect GPAs, elite college acceptance, or simply just looking matchy-matchy in our perfectly posed Facebook cover photo—we will recognize that the theme of refinement flows even in our own parenting.

More often than not presenting our children to the world in the very best light comes from pure desires. We want the very best for them because we love them deeply. We refine and perfect our children through discipline, instruction, and loving guidance. We understand that it's okay throw a temper tantrum on the floor because I won't let you touch the hot stove. We stand firm when our teenager slams her door, rolls her eyes loudly declaring us the "worst parents ever" because we won't allow her to go to the party where we know underage wisdom is fueled by alcohol and hormones. We apply time-out/in, we remove privileges, we issue chore lists, and we stick to "homework first, then play," even though, to our children, those things feel painful and frustrating. We do it because we know that when they are 30 they will, hopefully, appreciate it and be a productive member of society, repeating those same things to teach and instruct their next generation.

Oh how easily we forget that we, too, are children. Children of a perfect Father who loves us and knows that this pain, this frustration, this suffering will ultimately be for our good. We are born of the word of truth which is Jesus, as a first fruits of His ultimate sacrifice for

"Oh how easily we forget that we, too, are children. Children of a perfect Father who loves us and knows that this pain, this frustration, this suffering will ultimately be for our good."

us, a reflection of Him in all things—even suffering. I love the scripture from Malachi 3:1-3 (abridged), "I will send my messenger, who will prepare the way before me… but who can endure the day of his coming? Who can stand when he appears? For he will be like a refiner's fire…. He will sit as a refiner and purifier of silver."

I love the image of a biblical-time silversmith hovering with his head bowed over his work as he makes sure that the heat on the silver isn't too hot or too cool, but just the right amount of heat to bring the impurities (dross) to the top so that it can be removed. As he works diligently over his task, he carefully applies heat, removes dross, adjusts the heat, removes dross, repeats again and again until the silver is pure. How does the silversmith know it's pure? As he sits with head bowed over his work, the silver slowly—with every adjustment of heat and removal of dross—becomes clearer, until ultimately, it is like a mirror, and in its pureness can reflect his own image. What a powerful visual of our Heavenly Father's refinement of us through the heat of trial and suffering! He hovers over us, never allowing the heat to get too hot, or too cool. Through the pressure of trial, He slowly and methodically reveals our character and removes the dross. Repeating the process again and again as a proud Father, a refiner watching the reflection of Himself become clearer and clearer upon our life with every trial, with every frustration, with every moment. What a beautiful gift His refinement is toward us.

Scripture Meditation: Take a few moments to read the following Scriptures. Allow the Holy Spirit to speak to your heart about each of them.

Jeremiah 9:7 "Therefore, this is what the Lord of Heaven's Armies says: 'See, I will melt them down in a crucible and test them like metal. What else can I do with my people?'"

Read Malachi Chapter 3 in The Message Version.

Isaiah 48:10 "I have refined you, but not as silver is refined. Rather, I have refined you in the furnace of suffering."

Zechariah 13:9 "And I will bring the third part through the fire, refine them as silver is refined. And test them as gold is tested. They will call on My name, and I will answer them; I will say, 'They are My people' and they will say, 'The Lord is my God.'"

Capturing Thoughts: Throughout your adoption journey, I encourage you to capture your thoughts, fears, moments of joy, memories, and challenges. It will be a great encouragement to go back and read what you've written before. Looking back, you'll be surprised how much you and your family grow through your experiences.

Prayer Starter: Jesus, thank you that you set the perfect example of suffering for us. Willingly laying down your life and enduring accusation, shame, pain, and death on our behalf. As trial is present in our lives, help us to remember that we are being purified by it, and that on the other side we will be made more and more complete, perfect—lacking nothing. Help us to grow into your likeness and image so that we can reflect truth and love to our family, our community, and the world.

Discussion Questions – Day 18: Born of Truth

1. Have you ever made your children do something that they hated doing or something hard because you knew that ultimately it was something that was good for them? How does this parallel the work that Jesus might be doing

in your own life?

2. Read Malachi Chapter 3. How do you feel when your children honor you, even when they are frustrated or upset with you? How does that translate into how you honor and serve the Lord?

3. In today's devotion, Pam shared the description of a biblical silversmith refining silver. How does that image help you to better understand God's process of refinement in your life?

4. As you think about your children and their reflection of your family to the world, can you put that into perspective from God's viewpoint, with you as His child? How does that challenge or encourage you?

My Journey:

(Use this space to capture your thoughts, prayers, concerns and questions)

SO THEN, MY BELOVED BRETHREN, LET EVERY MAN BE SWIFT TO

HEAR, SLOW TO SPEAK, SLOW TO WRATH

JAMES 1:19

DAY 19: QUICK TO LISTEN

Ugh. That's kind of how I feel when I come to this scripture. I've been a total failure at listening, speaking or getting angry many times. It's so hard for me because I'm innately a problem solver, a fixer. Or, maybe a little bit of a control freak. God's still working on me, for sure. I've discovered something about myself in the process of learning to follow James' advice, I'm uncomfortable processing pain and sorrow. I'm also short-tempered. Ouch. This verse has been a huge wake up call to me and a huge mountain to overcome because I'm honestly just terrible at it. I'm forced to be very, very intentional; intentional to the point of having inner conversations with myself as I'm trying to have an outward interaction with someone else. It's because of my own need to work hard in this area that I want to take three days to talk about this one sentence in scripture. We cannot be too quick to slide past a verse that could literally be the difference between success or failure in our families. So, for the next three days I invite you to join me in discomfort and honesty. Here we go…

Have you seen the video of the little boy saying, "Listen, Linda…" to his mom over and over as he makes his case for a cupcake? Aside from the obvious parenting heartburn I experience when watching it, it's adorable and he's pretty persuasive. This is an echo of that inner voice in my head as I slow down to listen, really listen to others. "Listen, Pam. Pam, listen." Listening is a skill that we must cultivate if we want healthy relationships with others and with God. It's truly eye-opening to take a mental survey of yourself over a couple of days to see how much time you spend talking compared to how much time you spend listening.

I could tell you story after story of how I've gotten it wrong at listening, but for today, a simple story of getting it right was the most eye-opening moment of my life in terms of slowing down to listen. One of our daughters was at the dinner table with majorly negative attitude, which was actually out of character for her. I tried to ignore it at first, but her snarky remarks and general demeanor finally got to me and I simply said, "Would you like to be excused from the table and go to your room?" Her answer was a resounding, "Yes!" Off she went. After dinner was over and the clean up done, I went into her room and discovered her crying—which was also out of character for her. In a moment of clarity and "getting it right," I just calmly sat down on the bed beside her and asked, "Can you tell me what happened at the dinner table?" This was NOT a typical or natural response for me. On almost any other day I probably would have ordered her to her room, and not given her the option. I would have stormed into the room demanding to know why she thought it was okay to act that way at the dinner table. And, I probably would have gone in with an idea of consequences already on my mind. Thankfully, Jesus took the wheel.

After asking her to explain what was going on at dinner, I waited and patted her back while she cried. Finally, she sat up and apologized to me for her behavior and then went on to tell me one of the saddest things I've ever heard. She expressed that her behavior was driven by the scent of cantaloupe which I had cut up and placed in the center of the table as part of our dinner spread. The smell of it made her angry because she was immediately brought back to the memory of being a kid at home with her birth mother. When her mother was upset with her, she would smear cantaloupe in the carpet and make her eat it from the carpet fibers. Even writing this story now makes me want to tear up and cry for that precious little girl who today calls me mom in her mid-20s. As you can imagine, I'm so grateful, in this moment, I listened to her instead of focusing on my own frustration, what I wanted to say or how disrespectful her actions at dinner were. Can you imagine what I would have lost if I had missed this opportunity to listen? I would have totally lost the opportunity for my precious daughter to share her heart and her hurts. I would have missed a tremendous opportunity for understanding. I would have missed a moment of connection and vulnerability that didn't come easily for this child.

"You would be amazed at how much easier it is to ask for an explanation in a loving and inviting way when you're intentional in looking for the rest of the story."

Being quick to listen is a skill that requires us to remember that behind every action or reaction there's a story to be told. We need to be quick to listen so that we can understand what's really going on, rather than just what our assumption is about the event. As I've grown from that moment, I've tried to practice a simple technique of pausing and asking myself if there's something that I'm not seeing, counting to ten, and taking a breath. You would be amazed at how much easier it is to ask for an explanation in a loving and inviting way when you're intentional in looking for the rest of the story.

The art of listening is a gift that God gives us in teaching us to slow down and listen first to Him through His Word, and then to others as they share life with us. Although I didn't specifically touch on it in this devotion, the art of listening is also about being quick to listen to and accept correction, and to hear instruction. In this way, God brings us yet another gift of being humble to learn from others and grow. In big ways and small, the gift of listening brings us deeper understanding of others and helps us to grow in ways that our own ideas, and voices, never will.

As a follow up to the cantaloupe story, my sweet girl just sat down at family dinner with us recently and served herself cantaloupe! I looked at her in shock and said, "I can't believe you're eating cantaloupe." She said, "Jesus has healed that part of me." I gave her the biggest high five ever. I'm so proud of her and thankful to Jesus.

Scripture Meditation: Take a few moments to read the following Scriptures. Allow the Holy Spirit to speak to your heart about each of them.

> **Proverbs 1:5** "Let the wise hear and increase in learning, and the one who understands obtain guidance."

> **Matthew 11:15** "He who has ears to hear, let him hear."

> **Proverbs 21:23** "Whoever keeps his mouth and his tongue keeps himself out of trouble."

> **Ecclesiastes 3:7** "A time to tear, and a time to sew; a time to keep silence, and a time to speak."

Capturing Thoughts: Throughout your adoption journey, I encourage you to capture your thoughts, fears, moments of joy, memories, and challenges. It will be a great encouragement to go back and read what you've written before. Looking back, you'll be surprised how much you and your family grow through your experiences.

Prayer Starter: Father, help me to slow down and listen to others so that I can gain wisdom and understanding, especially for my children and family. Also forgive me for the times that I've missed and help me to make up for those lost opportunities at relationship building. Give me the ability to listen well to you, as my ultimate guide and teacher.

Discussion Questions – Day 19: Quick to Listen

1. In today's devotion, Pam tells a personal story about one of her daughter's behavior related to cantaloupe. As you read that story, how are you challenged to rethink some of your own children's behaviors?

2. Write down three ways that you could practice being a better listener. Share that list with a trusted friend or your spouse, and submit yourself to accountability in that area.

3. Has there ever been a time that you've felt like someone wasn't listening to you? Describe how you felt about your relationship with that person afterward.

4. Share a time that you did a great job of listening. How did it feel to get it right?

My Journey:

(Use this space to capture your thoughts, prayers, concerns and questions)

DAY 20: SLOW TO SPEAK

I like to talk, I like to debate, and I like to share my opinions. Sigh. The struggle is real. I might have permanent bite marks on the inside of my jaws from having to physically remind myself to wait to speak. My brain works fast and my mouth works faster, and the two aren't always in sync. They often move so fast that my heart doesn't even have a chance to get a word in edgewise. Sound familiar? If you're like me, this is probably the story of your life, in every relationship. Silence is hard, especially when I think there's so much that needs to be said.

Needless to say, this is an area that I still have a lot of room for growth in, and I still fail miserably at on a regular basis. Even so, it's also an area that I've grown in and that God is using to teach me some valuable things about relationships, especially with my daughters. Yesterday, I shared a story of success in listening. Today I'm sharing a story of failure in being slow to speak. I've already admitted to being a problem-solver and fixer, so this should come as no surprise to you.

Growing up I was the oldest of three siblings and our home was chaotic with my parents struggling with drugs, alcohol, anger, and mental illness. As a result, I became a peace-keeper and problem solver for our family and my little brothers. To this day, I'm often the one turned to in crisis or any major event because I push through the chaos and get things done, solve the problem, find the solution, and bring calm. I can't help it. Well, I can help it, it just takes lots of intentional effort. I've found that while these skills were necessary growing up (and they've been tremendously beneficial in my leadership and career), they aren't so great at home and in my closest relationships; a truth that one of my daughters made perfectly clear in a simple statement that rocked my world.

With eight daughters there is never a shortage of problems to be solved or crises to be averted. As mom, they come to me a lot to express their challenges and concerns. I fixed them. Or, I tried. Oh how I tried. Then one day, one of my precious ones said, "Mom, when I share a problem with you and you tell me three ways to solve it, I feel like that means you don't trust that I can solve it myself." Ouch. Double ouch. That was years ago and still, ouch. Her words rang deeply true. It was arrogant of me to think that the only reason for my kids to share their problems with me was so I, the master problem solver, could fix them. Not only was it arrogant, it was hurtful toward them. I apologized and tried clumsily to explain that my intention was never to make her feel like I didn't trust her. I'm not sure how sincere I sounded at the time since I was so shocked at the truth. I just hope that my actions since then have showed my sincerity. Since that conversation, I've practiced being slow to speak, gentle in my advice and questioning. "So what are you going to do about that?" "How can I help you with that?" "I have a couple of thoughts if you would like to hear them." That doesn't mean that there aren't still times that I'm not direct and quick with clear guidance. But I do intentionally try to honor their feelings and their autonomy in solving their own issues. They are more than capable and have surprised me in their ingenuity and insight. This hard-earned skill of mine has also drastically improved all of my relationships.

The other aspect of being slow to speak is that it gives us time to respond to a situation or point of conversation, rather than to simply react. I am a big believer in watching what we say and how we say it. Yes, you can always ask for forgiveness, but forgiveness doesn't come with a giant eraser attached. The words and feelings will always be remembered, even if they are forgiven. This is why it's so important to watch what we say, and how we say it.

> **"Yes, you can always ask for forgiveness, but forgiveness doesn't come with a giant eraser. The words and feelings will always be remembered, even if they are forgiven. "**

Learning to separate what needs to be said from what I want to say is a daily practice of walking closely with the Lord and asking Him to help me guard my tongue, a topic we will discuss in detail in a few days.

It is no coincidence listen and silent are both spelled with the same letters. These two words bring yesterday's theme together with today's, in order to truly listen we must first be silent. As maturing followers of Jesus Christ, our entire life is about becoming more and more like Him. The gift of God in being slow to speak is being like Jesus. It's not the number of words we speak that make a difference, it's the weight and wisdom of those words. The letters in black in my Bible far outnumber those in red, but those in red carry the wisdom of the world in them because they were His words.

Scripture Meditation: Take a few moments to read the following Scriptures. Allow the Holy Spirit to speak to your heart about each of them.

> **Proverbs 19:20** "Listen to advice and accept instruction, that you may gain wisdom in the future."

Exodus 14:14 "The Lord will fight for you, and you have only to be silent."

Romans 10:17 "So faith comes from hearing, and hearing through the word of Christ."

Philippians 2:3-4 "Do nothing from rivalry or conceit, but in humility count others more significant than yourselves. Let each of you look not only to his own interests, but also to the interest of others."

Luke 12:3 "Therefore whatever you have said in the dark shall be heard in the light, and what you have whispered in private rooms shall be proclaimed on the housetops."

Capturing Thoughts: Throughout your adoption journey, I encourage you to capture your thoughts, fears, moments of joy, memories, and challenges. It will be a great encouragement to go back and read what you've written before. Looking back, you'll be surprised how much you and your family grow through your experiences.

Prayer Starter: Lord, forgive me for speaking when I should be listening. Help me to become a better listener so that as I hear, truly hear, those around me I can respond to them with wisdom and love.

Discussion Questions – Day 20: Slow to Speak

1. Silence. It's certainly something we should practice more in life—in person, on social media, and in parenting. Do you speak too quickly or too often? If so, what can you do to be slower in speaking?

2. In what ways do you think slowing down before you speak might change your relationships with your family?

3. In today's devotion, Pam shared a story of one of her daughters talking about how she felt when sharing a problem. Take a moment and think about your last conflict with one of your children. How do you think they felt during the conflict? How does thinking about their feelings make you want to change your reactions and responses?

4. Read Philippians 2:3-4. In what ways does this scripture speak to you regarding your ability to be slower to speak?

My Journey:

(Use this space to capture your thoughts, prayers, concerns and questions)

DAY 21: SLOW TO ANGER

"I have one nerve left and you're jumping up and down on it." It's a funny phrase that I've used with my kids, and maybe my husband a time or two. "I'm going to count to three......1......2........2 and a half.......2 and three quarters.........thh...rrr....." We've all been there. On the verge of absolutely losing our marbles because we've had it. We're tired, we're overwhelmed, we feel disrespected, and our patience is so hair-thin that a gnat could trigger an explosion. We're not alone. There are multiple instances in the Old Testament that God's anger burned against the nation of Israel as they disobeyed Him time and time again. Yet, His patience and mercy are actually mind-boggling. If you've never read the Bible cover-to-cover, let that be a goal. It's intriguing (and frustrating) to watch God bless Israel, save them, provide for them and love them over and over again, and then watch them completely forget it all and do "whatever is right in their own sight" in direct defiance and disobedience. There are stories of quick judgment, stories of long-suffering patience, stories of mercy, and stories of forgiveness. God's journey with Israel is certainly reflection of parenting in general. It's hard. It is hard for God, and He is perfect. We (his children) are a hot

> **"God's journey with Israel is certainly a reflection of parenting in general. It's hard. It is hard for God, and He is perfect. We (his children) are a hot mess. "**

127

mess. Clearly, we're in trouble as parents because we are far from perfect.

This is especially important in the context of working with children who've experienced extreme trauma and loss; and who often suffer the effects of Post Traumatic Stress Disorder (PTSD) as a result of their history of abuse and neglect. If we express anger in the form of harsh words, tone of voice, facial expression, and body language, this can be a major trigger for our kids. It can force them into their fight-flight-freeze mode, and if we're honest about our own anger, we're probably operating in the same mode. In a conflict situation, you have two people who are operating out of what scientists refer to as our "reptilian brains"—the part of the brain that is simply about surviving. In order to survive, this primitive part of the brain shuts out the more advanced part of our brain where reasoning, understanding, and clear thinking reside. So you have two people fighting for their very survival against each other. That could get ugly pretty fast, for sure. If you're like me, as you read this description, a specific instance came to mind. I'll share.

I don't even remember what started the argument, but I clearly remember that it lasted for hours. Yes, I said hours. I can envision myself standing angry face to angry face with my 15-year-old daughter in an epic battle of wills and survival. We had both lost our marbles. She escalated, then I escalated. Game on. I was determined to win, and I did—but I didn't. She lost her phone and her going out privileges… because I am the mom and I have the power. I lost an opportunity to guide and correct, to love and connect. No matter, I won. After hours of epic screaming, silent treatment, storming out of the room and back in with an even better angry statement than the last one, and more than a few hot angry teary accusations, I finally made it into my bedroom, teenage phone in hand, and said to my husband, "Whew. That's finally over." He looked up from the book he was reading and said calmly, "I think you need a redo." Um. Wow. We're still married, and I still love him. He survived. He was right.

A "redo" is a concept taught by Dr. Karyn Purvis in her Trust Based Relational Intervention (TBRI) practice of connecting with our children who've experienced trauma and loss before correcting them. In connecting first, the simple objective is to bring the primal brain back in line with the thinking brain so that we can help them to calm down first, then address the behavior calmly, often playfully. A redo comes after we've restored balance and brain function and we give the child a chance to practice "getting it right." For more detailed understanding of this amazing practice, read *The Connected Child*, by Dr. Karyn Purvis. My loving, wonderful hubby was suggesting in six simple words that I had operated out of the wrong part of my brain and that my "win" was actually wrong and I needed to go back and make it right. The struggle is so real. I don't have enough eye rolls in me for how ridiculous my behavior felt.

I went back and apologized, discussed a more appropriate way to handle conflict in the future, and agreed on a more appropriate consequence. Y'all teenage girls are a force to be reckoned with, and even worse is their momma. Gah. All the hormones. My husband is a saint.

Being slow to anger would have certainly been a helpful mantra for me before heading into this conflict and many others like it. Over and over in Proverbs, Solomon reminds us that anger is foolish, impulsivity is dangerous, and short-temperedness results in broken relationships. Oh, but how quickly our pot can boil over. If we're not careful and intentional, our anger is disastrous.

I've often said to my kids, "I will always fight for you and sometimes I will fight with you because I believe in you so much." The motive and intention behind that statement is pure and good. I want the best for them, the absolute best. If it requires some arguments and conflict along the way, than so be it. That's life. Careful..... it's true, but it's a slippery slope because as we will discover tomorrow, anger doesn't produce the desired outcome we're seeking.

The gift that God is so graciously guiding us into as we've learned to be quick to listen, slow to speak and slow to anger is simple. It's the fruit of His spirit—patience, kindness, love, joy, peace, goodness, faithfulness, gentleness, and self-control. It's a refining gift, creating from within us a reflection that day by day is looking more and more like our Father.

Scripture Meditation: Take a few moments to read the following Scriptures. Allow the Holy Spirit to speak to your heart about each of them.

Proverbs 14:17 "A quick-tempered man acts foolishly, and a man of wicked intentions is hated."

Proverbs 14:29 "He who is slow to wrath has great understanding, but he who is impulsive exalts folly."

Proverbs 16:32 "He who is slow to anger is better than the mighty, and he who rules his spirit than he who takes a city."

Ecclesiastes 7:9 "Anger resides in the bosom of fools."

Capturing Thoughts: Throughout your adoption journey, I encourage you to capture your thoughts, fears, moments of joy, memories, and challenges. It will be a great encouragement to go back and read what you've written before. Looking back, you'll be surprised how much you and your family grow through your experiences.

Prayer Starter: Lord, forgive me for being quick to anger. Help me to develop the fruits of your Spirit so that in every relationship I am a representation of You, in all of your fullness. I want the relationship with my kids to last a lifetime and be full of good memories. I don't want them to remember me as an angry and stressed out parent. Help me to calm down and lean on you for discernment, patience, mercy, and grace.

Discussion Questions – Day 21: Slow to Anger

1. Today's devotions starts with, "I have one nerve left and you're jumping up and down on it." Have you ever found yourself saying something like this to your children? How easy or difficult is it for you to calm down when your emotions are high and you're angry?

2. What are some trigger points for you? As you identify them, write down a few ideas for how to remind yourself to stay calm when your own sensitive spots are triggered.

3. Pam shares a personal story about an argument with her daughter in which, by authority alone, she won. After her win, her husband pointed out that it wasn't a win at all and helped her to realize she had been wrong. Do you have a person in your life who can help you see where you're wrong when you behave badly? Share this devotion with them and ask them to keep you even more accountable in the area of quick anger.

4. How can you see God's spirit working in you in the area of anger? How can this group pray for you or help you?

My Journey:

(Use this space to capture your thoughts, prayers, concerns and questions)

DAY 22: WRATH & RIGHTEOUSNESS

Yesterday we talked about being slow to anger. Today, as James moves us forward, deeper into relationship with God, and more refined into His image, we learn a really profound reason to be slow to anger. It doesn't produce righteousness. It actually doesn't produce anything, it simply reproduces and multiplies the same—more wrath. I would venture a guess that this isn't the outcome you're looking to attain. Me either. It's vital we learn how to be intentional, even in moments of anger, so that over the long-haul we can bring about the ultimate goal in our own lives and the lives of our children, righteousness.

Sometimes random things show up at the perfect moments. My husband's uncle Carroll Parish, a pastor in Louisville, KY, just posted this statement on Facebook (yes, I take Facebook writing breaks) as I was typing today's devotion, "Sometimes we waste time and energy on things that produce very little." I couldn't have said it better myself. In anger we feel justified and we often have a goal of producing change in the other person, righteousness (right standing), and repentance. It simply doesn't work and is a total waste of our time and energy. How much better would our energy be spent if we took the time to lovingly correct and guide out of genuine understanding from a place of wisdom, because we've listened first, held our tongue and kept our emotions in place?

I want us to consider two sides of anger in this verse. First, the anger that's directed at our kids when dealing with them on any issue whether it's direct disobedience, poor behavior or general issues of annoyance. When acting out of this anger we feel justified to correct them because "they have to learn." It's true that they do need to learn and it is our responsibility to lead and guide them in righteousness; to teach them how to walk in right standing with the Lord, in society and within family. What James is saying here is that anger will not produce that result. It just won't. The truth is, most of the time anger is a result of our own needs and expectations not being met. If we truly stop to examine our anger, oftentimes it's selfish in nature—it's all about me. When we lash out at our children in anger, we tend to be overly critical and excessively harsh. We seek to issue swift punishment rather than training and correction. Our anger can also trigger fear and discouragement in our children. There are two companion verses to this one that clarify the reason that anger doesn't produce righteousness in our children: Ephesians 4:6, "Fathers, do not provoke your children to anger, bring them up in the discipline and instruction of the lord." And Colossians 3:21, "Fathers, do not provoke your children, lest they become discouraged." Put together the verses would read, "Fathers (parents), do not provoke your children to anger lest they become discouraged, but bring them up in the discipline and instruction of the Lord." Another translation ends Colossians 3:21 with this phrase, "lest he get discouraged and quit trying." None of us—not you, not me, not our children—respond to harshness well. Ever. In a calm moment, when we examine ourselves we're often mortified by our handling of a situation and can admit that we didn't come close to achieving the outcome we desired. I would venture to guess

> **"When we lash out at our children in anger, we tend to be overly critical and excessively harsh. We seek to issue swift punishment rather than training and correction."**

that anytime you've had those feelings as a parent, anger was involved. Our primary role in our children's lives is to steward them on behalf of God. They belong first to Him and have been temporarily given to us as a gift because He entrusts us to point them toward Him and demonstrate His love, character, grace, mercy, and kindness toward them. As we work with God in their development, we must submit our anger and frustrations to Him. We need to trust Him to give us the wisdom in each situation as we are quick to listen (to God and our children), slow to speak and slow to anger.

The second side of anger that I want to examine is what it does in our own lives. Over the past 22 days we've established that God's primary purpose for us is this life is to be refined into His image so that we can represent Him in fullness to a lost and dying world. He accomplishes this as we trust Him in patience and faith. Anytime we experience anger, the first thing that goes out the window is patience. Then our faith quickly follows as we lean solely on our own ability to handle the situation rather than trusting God and leaning into His wisdom. As a result, human wrath isn't producing righteousness in us either. The net result of anger acted out rather than prayed out is loss, for us and our children.

The gift that God has wrapped up for us is our own right standing before Him, and our children's. God's great kindness, patience, and love of us led us into relationship with Him. As His reflection on this earth toward our children, we are to use the same characteristics to guide them toward Him, so that, together, we can stand rightly before Him.

Scripture Meditation: Take a few moments to read the following Scriptures. Allow the Holy Spirit to speak to your heart about each of them.

Romans 2:1-5 "You may think you can condemn such people, but you are just as bad, and you have no excuse! When you say they are wicked and should be punished, you are condemning yourself, for you who judge others do these very same things. And we know that God, in his justice, will punish anyone who does such things. Since you judge others for doing these things, why do you think you can avoid God's judgment when you do the same things? Don't you see how wonderfully, kind, tolerant, and patient God is with you? Does this mean nothing to you? Can't you see that his kindness is intended to turn you from sin (to repentance)?"

Ephesians 4:26, 29-31 "In your anger, do not sin; do not let the sun go down while you are angry and don't give the devil a foothold. Do not let any unwholesome talk come out of your mouths, but only what is helpful for building up others according to their needs, that it may benefit those who listen. And do not grieve the Holy Spirit of God, with whom you were sealed for the day of redemption. Get rid of all bitterness, rage and anger, brawling and slander, along with every form of malice."

Proverbs 29:11 "Fools give full vent to their rage, but the wise bring calm in the end."

Ecclesiastes 7:9 "Do not be quickly provoked in your spirit, for anger resides in the lap of fools."

Capturing Thoughts: Throughout your adoption journey, I encourage you to capture your thoughts, fears, moments of joy, memories, and challenges. It will be a great encouragement to go back and read what you've written before. Looking back, you'll be surprised how much you and your family grow through your experiences.

Prayer Starter: Jesus, teach us to correct and guide our children in your ways with wisdom, not with anger. As we encounter the difficulties and exhaustion that often accompany parenting, give us the strength to lean on you and trust you so that we can have the patience to teach our children well and not to provoke them.

Discussion Questions – Day 22: Wrath & Righteousness

1. Have you ever experienced someone being harsh with you in anger? Talk about that experience and how it made you feel.

2. What is the number one way you act out in anger? Can you think of strategies to calm yourself in the future?

3. Today's devotion says, "The truth is, most of the time anger is a result of our own needs and expectations not being met. If we truly stop to examine our anger, oftentimes it's selfish in nature—it's all about me." Examine your needs and expectations that often lead you to anger.

4. Are there specific ways that you can be more patient with your child?

My Journey:

(Use this space to capture your thoughts, prayers, concerns and questions)

SO GET RID OF ALL THE FILTH AND EVIL IN YOUR LIVES, AND HUMBLY ACCEPT

THE WORD GOD HAS PLANTED IN YOUR HEARTS, FOR IT HAS THE POWER TO

SAVE YOUR SOULS.

JAMES 1:21

DAY 23: THROW IT AWAY

I walked into my kitchen the other day and immediately knew that there
was something going bad in my citrus bin. At first glance the bright orange
and yellow of my clementines and lemons looked beautiful and fresh, but
my sense of smell was telling me that something wasn't right. And if I
didn't find it and get rid of it, the rest of the fruit would suffer. After
digging a little bit, I felt the telltale softness of a rotting clementine. I
plucked it out of the group and examined the ones in closest proximity to it
to find out if the rotting had spread before getting rid of it in our compost
bin. Luckily the other ones were fine, but if I had put off getting rid of the
bad one, that wouldn't have been the case in 24 hours. The same is true of
the pieces of our own hearts and lives that are rotten and need to be gotten
rid of. If we aren't quick to act, those rotten parts effect everyone around
us, beginning with those in closest proximity—our family.

In the first part of today's scripture James exhorts us to get rid of all the
filth and evil in our lives, and at first glance most of us would
understandably want to brush off his admonition because it couldn't
possibly apply. He's talking to that "other" person we're thinking of right
now… you know….*that* one. Not so fast. He's talking to you, and to me.
Today we're going to pause and listen. We're going to get rid of it before it

139

spreads. So get your trash bag out and get ready to throw it all way.

Stealing, lying, murder, rape, slander, and the list goes on. When we think of wickedness, filth and evil, these are the things that come to mind, which make it super easy to excuse ourselves because, hopefully, none of these really apply. Oh what a dangerous way of thinking this is. Isaiah 64:6 applies the truth to this way of thinking, "We are all infected and impure with sin. When we display our righteous deeds, they

> **"It doesn't matter how good you are, your goodness still pales in comparison to God's and we are all given to sin and evil that lead us away from Him and into wickedness of heart and action."**

are nothing but filthy rags. Like autumn leaves, we wither and fall, and our sins sweep us away like the wind." It doesn't matter how good you are, your goodness still pales in comparison to God's and we are all given to sin and to evil that lead us away from Him and into wickedness of heart and action.

I was listening to a great teaching the other day from Bruce Wilkinson in which he talked about our refinement. In the teaching he shared that there are really three levels to our purity and regeneration before the Lord: our behavior, our character, and our motives. It's within these that we find the rotten fruit that must be thrown away. Let's talk about them one at a time.

First, our behaviors—what we do. We've dealt with lots of behavior over the past 23 days because our behavior is an outward indicator of an inward condition. I didn't have to cut open that clementine to discover that it was rotting on the inside, I could smell it and feel it. Our behavior is the same. When we lash out in anger, when we shut down, when we reject or ignore because our needs aren't being met, when we speak harshly, and when we exhibit any behavior that is the direct opposite of the fruits of the Spirit our outward actions are displaying our inward filth. It must be examined and gotten rid of, we must literally throw it away.

Second, our character—who we are. D.L. Moody describes character as "what you are in the dark." It is our thoughts, feelings, attitudes, dispositions, moral decisions and integrity that we give into behind the curtain when there's no one there but us. Years ago we went through a terrible foreclosure on our home. Even though we were in the middle of a short sale, the bank sold our home at auction and we were served with a thirty day notice that we could rent the property from the new owners, a rental company, or move. We moved into a rental home in our same neighborhood. Because our homes were both in close proximity to one another we decided to handle the move ourselves, one load at a time. It was exhausting. On our final night in the home, it was very late and I had divided the vacuuming of the floors and door/wall cleaning among our daughters and myself. In exhaustion one of my girls said, "Why do we have to even clean? It's not like we care what a company thinks about us." I paused. She was right, actually. The truth was that as a foreclosure, the company would probably come in the next day and rip everything out to do some needed renovations and our work would be lost. After pondering the thought for a moment, I gathered all of my girls on the staircase and said, "Look, I know you're tired and it may not make a lot of sense that we're cleaning this house at almost midnight when a company will likely come in and rip it all out anyway. But I want you to understand that leaving this house a disaster would not be integrity. Integrity isn't what you do when everyone's looking. It's what you do when no one will ever know. I don't care if no one ever walks in and appreciates that we left it spotless. God knows and we know. That's all that matters." One of my daughters repeats the phrase, "Integrity is what you do when no one is looking" all the time, to this day. Our character is the essence of who we are when no one is looking and that is why it is so critically important to keep whatever filth is inside of us cleaned out, because eventually (most of the time in intense trial) who we are comes out if we don't throw it out ahead of time.

Third, our motives—why we're doing it. The older I get, the more I realize how much of my life I've lived for the approval and acceptance of others—for my family, for my church, for my friends, for strangers that I will never know, and for ideals I've placed on myself driven by media or magazines. As I age and grow deeper in my relationship with the Lord, I realize that life is really about living for an audience of One, our Father in heaven. I love the line from Hillsong United's *From the Inside Out*, "Everlasting, your light will shine when all else fades. Never ending, your glory goes beyond all fame." It reminds me of the day that's coming for all of us when the trappings of this world will be stripped away and all we are and all we've done will be laid bare before the God of creation as we stand before Him accountable. It's imperative that we ask ourselves, whatever we're doing in life, if we're doing it to look good in front of others or to stand approved before our God.

You see, my friends, the gift God is giving us is time. Time to root out all evil lurking within us, to lay aside our own wickedness so we can come before Him pure, and holy; a grateful and gorgeous child into the presence of our Loving Father.

Scripture Meditation: Take a few moments to read the following Scriptures. Allow the Holy Spirit to speak to your heart about each of them.

Galatians 5:22-23 "But the fruit of the Spirit is love, joy, peace, patience, kindness, goodness, faithfulness, gentleness, self-control; against such things there is no law."

Colossians 3:12-15 "Put on then, as God's chosen ones, holy and beloved, compassionate hearts, kindness, humility, meekness, and patience, bearing with one another and, if one has a complaint against another, forgiving each other; as the Lord has forgiven you, so you also must forgive. And above all else put on love, which binds everything together in perfect harmony. And let the peace of Christ rule in your hearts, to which indeed you were called in one body. And be thankful."

Matthew 12:35 "The good person out of his good treasure brings forth good, and the evil person out of his evil treasure brings forth evil."

Titus 1:15-16 "To the pure, all things are pure, but to the defiled and unbelieving, nothing is pure; but both their minds and their consciences are defiled. They profess to know God, but they deny him by their works. They are detestable, disobedient, unfit for any good work."

Capturing Thoughts: Throughout your adoption journey, I encourage you to capture your thoughts, fears, moments of joy, memories, and challenges. It will be a great encouragement to go back and read what you've written before. Looking back, you'll be surprised how much you and your family grow through your experiences.

Prayer Starter: Father, purify our hearts, our motives, our character, and our behaviors. Reveal to us anything that is unclean within us and give us the wisdom and understanding to remove it from our lives. Help us to walk in right standing before you so that we can serve you and our family, in health and holiness.

Discussion Questions – Day 23: Throw it Away

1. Has a major trial ever revealed a character flaw in you that you were unaware of? If so talk about how you dealt with it once you saw it.

2. What's the hardest thing about accepting the idea that our own goodness is still filthy in comparison to God's goodness?

3. Read Colossians 3:12-15. What does it mean to "put on" these characteristics? How do we allow the peace of Christ to rule our hearts? Are you thankful right now?

4. In today's devotion Pam shares a story about teaching her children integrity. Can you recall a time that you were taught or you taught your child a profound character truth? Share it with the group.

My Journey:

(Use this space to capture your thoughts, prayers, concerns and questions)

SO GET RID OF ALL THE FILTH AND EVIL IN YOUR LIVES, AND HUMBLY ACCEPT

THE WORD GOD HAS PLANTED IN YOUR HEARTS, FOR IT HAS THE POWER TO

SAVE YOUR SOULS.

JAMES 1:21

DAY 24: RECEIVE THE WORD

One of the skills I've been trying to cultivate lately as a leader and parent is active listening—responding instead of reacting. In the process of learning to be a better listener, I've been researching Improv Comedy skills. If you think about Improv, each comedian has a responsibility to keep the comedic bit moving—regardless of what their partner says. It's definitely a skill that's easy to think of as "natural." Yet, most successful Improv comedians will tell you that they practice all the time. That practice includes being a very attuned and active listener, prepared to take a hook from whatever has been said and run with it. In Improv, it doesn't really matter what you *want* to say and there is no way to prepare beforehand. You simply have to suspend your mind's desire to do its own thing and participate actively as a part of the team, subject to whatever direction your partners go. A key to being good at Improv is the ability to find the "hook" in whatever your partner says and respond with acceptance and move on. If your partner randomly starts out with purple unicorns dressed in camo, you suspend your mind and accept their direction to keep the skit moving. Purple unicorns dressed in camo? Yes! I can see them now as they prance through the woods, bringing magical dreams to the little girl living in the hollow stump at the center of the forest, undetected by the ever-watchful eyes of the dream-stealing owl. And the story continues. The key for each person in an Improv setting is to not block the story, but accept the direction and keep it moving. The same is true as we receive the Word of God into our lives, we must suspend our mind's desire to control our lives and accept that God's direction is the best. It takes practice and humility.

In the second part of today's verse James, admonishes us to "humbly accept the Word that God has planted in our heart, for it has the power to save your soul." Other versions say to "receive with meekness the implanted word…" The key to receiving the Word of God and allowing its power to manifest in our lives is demonstrating humility and meekness. The original wording portrays the image of bending down to intently examine something to gain understanding. This is how we must approach the Word of God—intently, to gain understanding. Our hearts must be humble and teachable. Like our Improv comedian in the earlier example, we must be willing to accept what God is saying and act on it, without changing it to suit our own desires or plans. Being willing to learn with humility requires us to sit before God as a child and listen intently to the story He's writing in our lives through His Word. When I think of our posture before the Lord in receiving His Word, I think of kindergarteners gathered around their teacher on the story-mat listening wide-eyed as her voice teaches, instructs and entertains them. I imagine us sitting attentively with the Word before us or listening closely as the Word is spoken, like a child soaking up every word as truth, without argument. This type of humility requires a softness of heart and a reverence (fear) of the Lord that opens our minds to understanding and knowledge.

"Being willing to learn with humility requires us to sit before God as a child and listen intently to the story He's writing in our lives through His Word."

As we humbly accept the Word of the Lord, it becomes implanted in our hearts and begins to bear fruit. We planted a garden a few weeks ago and about a week after planting, I saw a section of soil bulging as the tiny seed was growing beneath it ready to burst through into the light and sprout upward as a giant sunflower. The Word is like that in our hearts; it sits as a seed, growing underneath the surface and developing a solid root system so that, when the time is right, it can burst forth in light and produce goodness, kindness, love, patience, peace, self-control, and all of the fruits of the Spirit.

In positioning our hearts humbly and meekly before the Lord, we soften our inner man and receive the greatest gift of all: the Spirit of the Living God alive within us, armed with the Truth of the Word. It's out of this gift that we are able to give birth to light, healing, and joy in the midst of our families.

Scripture Meditation: Take a few moments to read the following Scriptures. Allow the Holy Spirit to speak to your heart about each of them.

> **Luke 8:15** "And the seeds that fell on the good soil represent honest, good-hearted people who hear God's word, cling to it, and patiently produce a huge harvest."

> **Colossians 2:6** "And now, just as you accepted Christ Jesus as your Lord, you must continue to follow him."

> **Matthew 4:4** "But Jesus told him, 'No! The Scriptures say, People do not live by bread alone, but by every word that comes from the mouth of God.'"

John 17:17 "Make them holy by your truth; teach them your word, which is truth."

Capturing Thoughts: Throughout your adoption journey, I encourage you to capture your thoughts, fears, moments of joy, memories, and challenges. It will be a great encouragement to go back and read what you've written before. Looking back, you'll be surprised how much you and your family grow through your experiences.

Prayer Starter: Lord, forgive us where we've been hard-hearted and hard-headed toward your Word. Holy Spirit help us to have meek and tender hearts to the Word of God so that it can be buried deep within our hearts and produce the fruits of life in our family.

Discussion Questions – Day 24: Receive the Word

1. Do you read the Word like a child, with anticipation and eagerness to learn and apply it? Talk about your reading habits.

2. What is your biggest takeaway from today's devotion? What might you change as a result?

3. Read Luke 8:15. What does this passage of scripture mean to you?

4. In today's devotion Pam shares the analogy of Improv comics and the need to practice active listening and participation. In what ways can you practice better listening? How can you use the example of Improv comedy skills to improve your communication with God and others?

My Journey:

(Use this space to capture your thoughts, prayers, concerns and questions)

DAY 25: DO WHAT YOU'VE HEARD

I love this verse. The depth of its truth was first taught to me by my pastor, Dennis Rouse. It's his life verse. He often tells the story of finding this verse and the Holy Spirit revealing to Him that in order to accomplish all that God has set aside for him to accomplish, this must be a cornerstone of his life: to not just read the word and understand it, but to put it into action. Over the past thirty years, he's done just that. He and his wife Colleen founded Victory World Church, and together, they built one of the nation's largest multi-cultural churches, right in the center of the deep south with more than 13,000 people representing 110 different nationalities, who come together every week and worship side by side. Every time I read this verse, I think his faithfulness to act on the Word of God that was implanted in his heart and about the visible fruit of that obedience. If you want to fully understand what applying the Word to your life as a *doer* looks like, I encourage you to visit victoryatl.com and look up the sermon series that Dennis recently taught titled *"10."* It's a series based on his recent book by the same title in which he shares the ten qualities that move us from being believers (hearers only) to disciples (doers who put the Word into action). You won't regret it.

What does James mean when he says to be a doers of the Word (putting the Word in action)? He means take action! Don't just read this devotional, walk away patting yourself on the back because you've "done your time"

151

with the Lord today and then change nothing within yourself or your family. Don't just go to church, raise your hands in worship, say "Amen" to every word the pastor says and then not think about God, worship or honor Him for another seven days. This is where the rubber meets the road in our maturity in Christ. In Matthew Chapter 19, March Chapter 10, and Luke Chapter 18, there is a rich young ruler who asks Jesus what he must do for eternal life because he thinks that by just following what he's heard, he's safe. When Jesus challenges him to put the Word into action by laying aside the comforts of his life, he walks away unchanged and unwilling. Like the greed that lay in the young man's heart under all of his piety, each of us have areas of our life that we protect and value. Just as it did with the young ruler, the Word can expose those areas in us, and we have to decide what to do with what we've heard.

People often look at our story, starting as a family of three with a precious 11-year-old daughter and adding seven more daughters through foster care and adoption over an eight year period, and they ask, "How did your biological daughter respond?" Or, in the midst of those eight years they would ask, "What is this doing to your *real* daughter?" First, all of our daughters are *real* to us. Second, it was hard. Super hard. I can't even touch on those areas right now, but if you haven't read my first two devotionals, *Ready or Not* and *Battle-Weary Parents*, I encourage you to pick them up. More of the story of our family's journey is shared there. For this topic this is what I will say: our "Yes" was to God alone in obedience to His Word. Period. Many times along the way when doubt would creep in through the voice of a well-meaning friend, we would have to go back to God's Word and to prayer. He always, always confirmed His Word. We simply made the decision, over and over, to be *doers* in obedience and faith. I'm so thankful that we did.

One day each one of us will stand before the Lord and He will not ask us what we knew about him, but what we did with what we knew. We will stand before the ultimate judge as He examines the fruit of our lives lived in obedience to His Word on the earth. As an American I look around at the comforts of our lives and the accessibility of the Word and the Church to us, and I am frightened by the level of accountability to which we will be held on that day. It's easy for the enemy of our souls to fool us into thinking that weekly church attendance and whispered prayers of provision are enough. They are not. Too many people spend their whole lives marking up their Bibles while failing to allow the Bible to mark their lives.

> **"It's easy for the enemy of our souls to fool us into thinking that weekly church attendance and whispered prayers of provision are enough."**

To close today's devotion I want to share a story that I heard about a preacher who had just ended his Sunday service. As he stood at the exit of the church greeting congregants as they left, one man said, "That was a great sermon!" The pastor shook his hand and replied, "That remains to be seen." The greatness of the sermon will only be determined by the action it produces in the man's heart and life. Will he go away and do what he's heard? Will you?

The gift that we are unwrapping today is the gift of action. To begin taking everything we're learning about God through His Word and putting it into action in our lives and in our families. Like that great Switchfoot song lyric, I dare you to move.

Scripture Meditation: Take a few moments to read the following Scriptures. Allow the Holy Spirit to speak to your heart about each of them.

Luke 11:28 "Jesus replied, 'But even more blessed are all who hear the word of God and put it into practice."

John 13:17 "Now that you know these things, God will bless you for doing them."

Matthew 28:20 "Teach these new disciples to obey all the commands I have given you. And be sure of this: I am with you always, even to the end of the age."

Romans 2:13 "For merely listening to the law doesn't make us right with God. It is obeying the law that makes us right in his sight."

Capturing Thoughts: Throughout your adoption journey, I encourage you to capture your thoughts, fears, moments of joy, memories, and challenges. It will be a great encouragement to go back and read what you've written before. Looking back, you'll be surprised how much you and your family grow through your experiences.

Prayer Starter: Father, give us the strength to do what your Word has instructed us to do. Help us to fight the deceiver of our souls and not to settle for "good enough" in our walk with you. Thank you for your Word and its power to transform us from the inside out. We're grateful that you've entrusted us with your Spirit and given us the gifts, courage, and abilities to impact our family and our world for you.

Discussion Questions – Day 25: Do What You've Heard

1. In today's devotion, Pam says, "One day each one of us will stand before the Lord and He will not ask us what we knew about him, but what we did

with what we knew. We will stand before the ultimate judge as He examines the fruit of our lives lived in obedience to His Word on the earth." What emotions, fears, and challenges does this statement create for you?

2. Think about the rhythm of your daily life. How much do you actively think about being a doer of the Word?

3. Pam shares the story of growing her family through obedience to God alone. How easy is it for you to remember that your role in foster care and adoption is to be obedient to God's Word?

4. Talk about being comfortable in routine Christianity. How can you shake things up a bit in your own life?

My Journey:

(Use this space to capture your thoughts, prayers, concerns and questions)

DAY 26: LOOKING IN THE MIRROR

Snapchat. Instagram. Facebook. Twitter. There are oh so many places to project our image. It seems these days that no one is really afraid of the camera lens, our modern day mirror. The problem is that it lies, or rather we can change the feedback we're getting. We must hold the camera at a certain angle. Tuck this in and stick that out. Stand a certain way and pucker our lips just so. I've even known one of my girls to sit in a car with the air vent blowing so she can get a "wind-blown" look. I haven't even mentioned the filters yet. We can filter and face-tune out any flaw. And, honestly, if we are truly unhappy with what we see, we can just delete it. But you know what doesn't lie? A mirror—a real one.

Recently on a family trip one of my grandsons began running around asking everyone, "You know what you look like?" It was hilarious because in his six-year-old brain he was passing along a funny joke, but he didn't get how the punch-line worked, so he would choose any random object in his sight and then cackle at himself for how perfect his zinger was. My favorite was when he looked at his Aunt Kristan and said, "You know what you look like?" and she said, "What?" He looked quickly around and saw a red plastic cup and said enthusiastically, "You look like a cup!" Then he cupped his hands over his mouth, crinkled his little eyes, and snickered at his own genius. To this day, we will still look at each other and say, "You know what you look like?" and follow with the cup line, hand motions, and a cute little snicker. This is the question James wants us to ask ourselves as we look deeper into the mirror of the Word.

Do you know what you look like? As followers of Jesus Christ, the Word of God invites us into an honest assessment of ourselves. This verse is central to our entire walk with the Lord. Are we willing to allow the Word to be a mirror and use it to identify our flaws so that we might change them? Like a mirror, we must use the Word to verify that what we think we look like is actually true. We've all looked in a mirror in horror as we discover spinach from our morning omelet in our teeth or a forgotten zipper. Each time we think, "Why didn't someone tell me?!" Well, let me be your someone today and tell you that you need to go check yourself in the mirror. There's something there. It's true for all of us.

The Word of God reveals who we are. Not our filtered version of reality, but the real us, warts and all. Just like we wouldn't walk out of the house without checking ourselves in the mirror, we should never go through a day without checking our soul in the mirror of the Word. Through a disciplined practice of observing ourselves in its reflection, we can purify our hearts and minds, giving us the ability to stand before God without spot or

> ## "The Word of God reveals who we are. Not our filtered version of reality, but the real us, warts and all."

blemish on the day that's coming for all of us. It also gives us the ability to accomplish all that is set before us right now in our families and the world by removing the obstacles of our own imperfection through the washing of the Word.

The Word is a reflection of God's perfect love, perfect character, and perfect redemption. As we submit to all it is in our lives, our imperfections are made apparent giving us the gift of truth and allowing us to bring correction to our lives.

Scripture Meditation: Take a few moments to read the following Scriptures. Allow the Holy Spirit to speak to your heart about each of them.

> **Hebrews 4:12-13** "For the word of God is alive and powerful. It is sharper than the sharpest two-edged sward, cutting between the soul and spirit, between joint and marrow. It exposes our innermost thoughts and desires. Nothing in all creation is hidden from God. Everything is naked and exposed before his eyes, and he is the one to whom we are accountable."

> **Matthew 7:21-23** "Not everyone who calls out to me, 'Lord! Lord!' will enter the Kingdom of Heaven. Only those who actually do the will of my Father in heaven will enter. On judgment day many will say to me, 'Lord! Lord! We prophesied in your name and cast out demons in your name and performed many miracles in your name.' But I will reply, 'I never knew you. Get away from me, you who break God's laws.'"

> **1 Timothy 4:8** "Physical training is good, but training for godliness is much better, promising benefits in this life and in the life to come."

> **1 Corinthians 4:4** "My conscience is clear, but that doesn't prove I'm right. It is the Lord himself who will examine me and decide."

Capturing Thoughts: Throughout your adoption journey, I encourage you to capture your thoughts, fears, moments of joy, memories, and challenges. It will be a great encouragement to go back and read what you've written before. Looking back, you'll be surprised how much you and your family grow through your experiences.

Prayer Starter: Jesus, I can't thank you enough for your perfect Word that is a mirror into my imperfect heart. Give me the humility to allow you to reveal the areas that I can improve and show me where my human faults are stumbling blocks along my own path.

Discussion Questions – Day 26: Looking in the Mirror

1. Do you know what you look like? Pam uses a cute story of her grandson to illustrate this life-altering question. When was the last time that you allowed the Word to reveal an area that needs improvement in your life?

2. Read Hebrews 4:12-13. The passage is talking about the power of God's word to reveal even our innermost thoughts and desires. Are there things that you have kept hidden? Can you confess them to the Lord and to someone you trust?

3. Do you have a dedicated time that you spend with the Lord? If so, talk about how that benefits your life. If not, talk about the challenges that prevent this and how you can overcome them.

4. Has there been a time in your life when you've experienced a radical change as a result of the Word acting as a mirror in your life? If so, share this experience with the group.

My Journey:

(Use this space to capture your thoughts, prayers, concerns and questions)

DAY 27: FORGETTING OURSELVES

I'm in my mid-forties and my brain just ain't what it used to be. There was a time in my life when I could remember almost anything. My husband has always been a list-maker and a "trap-setter" saying, "If I don't make a list or leave this here as a trap, I won't remember it." I've always rolled my eyes and frustratingly stepped over yet another pile of stuff laying randomly in the center of the floor. If this were a text I would use the short text of "SMH" or, "shaking my head." At myself. Like a good Jedi Master, he has now taught me the wisdom of his ways, despite the times that I, as a young Padawan, scoffed at them. Almost daily, I now have to consult my list because I've forgotten something that I need to do. Also, much to my chagrin, I've adopted my grandfather's practice of "putting this away where I won't forget it" and not being able to find it. Truth be told, there's still a Christmas present for one of my grandsons in this house "put away where I won't forget it" and I haven't found it in months. Poor kid, it's a good thing he was too young to realize he was a gift short on Christmas Day. Oh well, when I find it, I'll be one gift ahead for this Christmas.

This is exactly the kind of thing that James is talking about in today's scripture. Yesterday we learned that we have to see ourselves in the mirror of the Word. Today, he carries that instruction forward and tells us that after we've been made aware of who we really are, we must not forget ourselves. How many times have we listened to a great sermon on anger, only to walk out into the church parking lot afterward and honk at, yell at and berate the driver in front of us who is letting out every car known to man before moving on? Seriously, what on earth? All the good stuff at Golden Corral's buffet will be gone if we don't hurry. Or how many times have we listened to some great wisdom on parenting only to walk back through our front door and start yelling like a banshee at our precious ones, sending everyone into eternal time-out because… well, just because? Bless our hearts.

If we aren't careful to apply the Word (be a doer), our lives look like a colander. When we're immersed in the water (the Word, a church service, etc.) we appear full, but remove us from that environment and everything we've learned leaks away and we forget what we've learned. The word "forget" can also mean to neglect or disregard. This is an indication of a heart attitude that is not teachable. We hear truth, but we disregard it because we don't want to make that change or we disagree. It's understandable. Anytime we see something in ourselves that we don't like, we don't necessarily want to keep thinking about it. If something makes us uncomfortable, it's much easier to shift our thinking and focus to something more pleasant and, in time, forget the discomfort all together.

> **"We hear truth, but we disregard it because we don't want to make that change, or we disagree."**

And although this is natural and understandable, it's still dangerous in our walk with the Lord. This type of behavior stalls us out and prevents us from stepping forward into the fullness of life that God has designed for us to live.

In the foster care and adoption world, there is so much wisdom to be gained on how to parent children from hard places and understand their trauma. The challenge with this wisdom is that it often flies in the face of traditional parenting methods which are often punitive in nature. So many times after I've taught a seminar, I hear parents totally dismiss the wisdom of a technique because it seems "too lenient" or "too silly," it "won't work on my kid," or a thousand other reasons. I watch them as they walk out of the session and think, "Their situation may never change because they don't want to hear the truth and apply it in their homes." The sad fact is, many times I've been in their shoes. Especially when the changing is mine to do. Many times when we are learning from experts or other parents, they are serving as our mirror into the things that can be improved in our homes. Just like James admonishes in today's scripture, we mustn't see ourselves, walk away and forget (neglect or disregard) what we've seen. We have to put it into action in our lives and in our homes.

The gift of intentional awareness and application of wisdom to our life is truly a gift that keeps on giving. As we learn to see ourselves and our flaws in the light of hope and through the lens of our Hope-Giver, we see the beauty in change and growth. In forgetting ourselves, we can remember Jesus and His great love for us. From this place we can love our families well and put our trust in Him.

Scripture Meditation: Take a few moments to read the following Scriptures. Allow the Holy Spirit to speak to your heart about each of them.

> **1 Corinthians 11:1-2** "Be imitators of me, just as I also am of Christ. Now I praise you because you remember me in everything and hold firmly to the traditions, just as I delivered them to you."

> **Mark 4:15** "The seed that fell on the footpath represents those who hear the message, only to have Satan come at once and take it away."

Romans 10:16 "But not everyone welcomes the good news. For Isaiah says, 'Lord, who has believed our message?'"

1 Timothy 4:16 "Pay close attention to yourself and to your teaching; persevere in these things, for as you do this you will ensure salvation both for yourself and for those who hear you."

Capturing Thoughts: Throughout your adoption journey, I encourage you to capture your thoughts, fears, moments of joy, memories, and challenges. It will be a great encouragement to go back and read what you've written before. Looking back, you'll be surprised how much you and your family grow through your experiences.

Prayer Starter: Lord, seal your Word in our hearts. Give us the desire to take action on the truth that you reveal to us through your Word and through the wisdom and experience of others. Holy Spirit help us to welcome the good news in our lives so that it might bring healing, change, and hope into our family.

Discussion Questions – Day 27: Forgetting Ourselves

1. Have you ever heard an instruction or correction that you didn't like and decided to ignore it? Talk about the outcome of that decision.

2. Mark 4:15 says, "The seed that fell on the footpath represents those who hear the message, only to have Satan come at once and take it away." How does this portion of scripture apply to today's devotion? How does this sometimes represent your life?

3. What are some of the best pieces of advice or wisdom you've ever received in foster care or adoption? Share those with the group.

4. Take time to quietly journal some things you need to intentionally apply.

My Journey:

(Use this space to capture your thoughts, prayers, concerns and questions)

BUT HE WHO LOOKS INTO THE PERFECT LAW OF LIBERTY AND CONTINUES IN IT,
AND IS NOT A FORGETFUL HEARER, BUT A DOER OF THE WORK, THIS ONE WILL
BE BLESSED IN WHAT HE DOES.

JAMES 1:25

DAY 28: BLESSED IN WHAT YOU DO

Oh how I love Jesus. I write that sentence in full reverence and love for the
Lord who has saved me, redeemed me, and turned the ashes of my life into
beauty. The background music as I type this is a version of Amazing Grace
my husband is playing in the same room, a heavy metal version. Heavy
metal or not, I am blessed to have a husband who loves the Lord and me.
One look at the recent texts on my phone fills me with gratitude at God's
blessings. None of our daughters are currently living at home. They are all
out kicking the adult life's booty. But today alone, I've texted with almost
all of them, or had a conversation, shared a funny meme or responded to a
prayer request. I've heard "I love you! I'm proud of you, mom!" I've said,
"I love you so much! I'm so proud of you." I've gotten texts of excitement,
texts of the mundane, and text of disappointment. Do you know how long
I've prayed for these relationships with my adult daughters, and still do?
Daily. That has been and still is my prayer, every day, for as long as I've
known each of them. I'm so blessed that my prayers are being answered.
That doesn't mean it's sunshine and roses every day; it's not. But we are a
family and we're still in it together, through thick and thin.

When I look back at all the ways that the enemy tried to rip apart the fabric
of our family, I'm moved to tears. When I think about that *Battle-Weary
Parent* that I've been so many times—so close to throwing my hands up in

defeat—my faith is encouraged and energized, remembering God's absolute faithfulness in the darkest moments. When I think about the tears, the prayers, the fears, and the failures, I'm humbled and in awe of my God who hears me when I pray and sends answers. There's no better word that I would use to describe how I feel about my life, even though it's far from easy or perfect, than "blessed." I truly feel like I'm blessed in what I do.

This verse so perfectly begins to bring this chapter and what we've learned over the last few weeks to a clos—looking into the perfect law of God and continuing in it through trial, counting it all a joy. Exercising our patience in understanding we are perfect and complete in Him, lacking nothing. Asking for wisdom without doubt and trusting in Him alone despite the storms and the waves. Understanding that when God seems silent, He is still there—and faithfully continuing. Standing in stability on His truth and direction for our lives. Facing trial and knowing that it's for our purification and regeneration, to earn the crown of life. Facing the temptations that the enemy of our souls places in our path by not allowing our desires to give birth to sin and death. Keeping ourselves from deception by keeping our gaze on the good and perfect gift of our God, the Father of Lights. Being swift to hear, slow to speak, and slow to anger because we understand that our anger doesn't produce righteousness. Laying aside our own wickedness so that we can become teachable and receive the Word of God. Putting into action the Word that has been implanted in us, as we gaze upon ourselves in the mirror, not walking away and forgetting what we've learned. In this, God promises blessing in all we do.

> **"Serving God in obedience even when it looks like everything is falling apart is anything but easy. Even so, it is worth it. It's a gift."**

I love the phrase, "Hindsight is always 20/20." It's so very true. As I look back on my life in the past 10 years, I'm astounded at the blessings of God that have been birthed through obedience and prayer. I didn't always see God's hand at work in the midst of my struggle, but in hindsight I see it so clearly. Serving God in obedience even when it looks like everything is falling apart is anything but easy. Even so, it is worth it. It's a gift.

Scripture Meditation: Take a few moments to read the following Scriptures. Allow the Holy Spirit to speak to your heart about each of them.

Philippians 4:9 "And my God will meet all your needs according the riches of his glory in Christ Jesus."

Isaiah 41:10 "So do not fear, for I am with you; do not be dismayed, for I am your God. I will strengthen you and help you; I will uphold you with my righteous right hand."

Psalm 23:1-4 "The Lord is my shepherd, I lack nothing. He makes me lie down in green pastures, he leads me beside quiet waters, he refreshes my soul. He guides me along the right paths for his name's sake. Even though I walk through the darkest valley, I will fear no evil, for you are with me; your rod and your staff, they comfort me."

2 Samuel 22:3-4 "My God is my rock, in whom I take refuge, my shield and the horn of my salvation. He is my stronghold, my refuge and my savior—from violent people you save me. I called to the Lord, who is worthy of praise, and have been saved from my enemies."

Capturing Thoughts: Throughout your adoption journey, I encourage you to capture your thoughts, fears, moments of joy, memories, and challenges.

It will be a great encouragement to go back and read what you've written before. Looking back, you'll be surprised how much you and your family grow through your experiences.

Prayer Starter: Father, thank you for the blessing that you've placed upon my life. Help me daily to remember to be grateful for the very breath in my lungs that gives me the ability to walk with you another day. Help me to remember, even in darkness, that you are always there and you are bringing order out of my chaos and calm to my storm.

Discussion Questions – Day 28: Blessed in What You Do

1. In today's devotion Pam celebrates all that God has done in her family. When was the last time you took some time to truly feel gratitude toward God and express it back to Him? If you haven't in a while, take a moment and tell Him.

2. Psalm 23:1-4. As a scripture we are accustomed to hearing, we often overlook the deep meaning in David's words. Read this scripture aloud and talk about its meaning to you.

3. Hindsight being 20/20, what prayers has God answered in your family? Share them with the group as an encouragement to one another.

4. As you read the summary paragraph of everything that's been covered in this devotion so far, did a nearly complete picture begin to form around what a person wholeheartedly devoted to the Lord would look like?

My Journey:

(Use this space to capture your thoughts, prayers, concerns and questions)

IF ANYONE AMONG YOU THINKS HE IS RELIGIOUS, AND DOES NOT BRIDLE HIS
TONGUE BUT DECEIVES HIS OWN HEART, THIS ONE'S RELIGION IS USELESS.

DAY 29: USELESS RELIGION

After yesterday, you might have been tempted to think James was finally
done with the hard stuff. Not so fast. Today and tomorrow, as we close out
James Chapter 1 and our 30 days of immersion in this scripture, James
brings us to a juxtaposition of two statements: today's verse and the most
famous verse in all of foster care and adoption, James 1:27. The essence of
the two verses boils down to false religion and pure religion. The difference
between the two is the test of true heart transformation. In the original text,
James used two versions of the same word that have been translated into
the singular word "religion" in our modern Bibles. In verse 26, he uses the
word *threskos*, an adjective, and in verse 27, he uses the word *threskeia*, a
noun. In other words, it's the difference between who you portray
(describe) yourself to be and who you actually are (your true identity), as
evidenced by the actions of your life.

I heard a story once of Bishop Taylor Smith sitting at his barber shop,
explaining to his barber that faith in Christ alone was all he needed to be
saved. The barber had sharp objections and said that he was doing his best
to serve God, and that was good enough. When the barber finished his
haircut, the bishop got up, and another man sat in his place. The bishop
then turned and asked the barber if he could do the man's haircut, to which
the barber exclaimed, "No, you aren't a barber." "But," the bishop replied,
"I'll do the best I can." The barber replied, "But your best is not good
enough." Even our best efforts aren't good enough to earn us salvation. If

you truly stop and consider the price Jesus paid for us on the Cross, you will realize the level of humility it requires to accept and believe. To recognize that everything we've been given in this life (and the one to come) as sons and daughters of God is because of another man's sacrifice. The fact that we can't earn it though our own worth, good deeds, or efforts is a hard pill to swallow for some. This is the crux of the matter for James in this verse. Don't think just because you do all the religious activities and look good to others, that you're truly honoring God. Our knowledge of God and outward acts of piety are self-deception if they don't originate from a place of humility, acknowledging Jesus and His work alone as the only transformative force in our lives and the lives of our family members.

Our tongue, the example used here, is an outward reflection of our inward soul's health. He's talking about self-control and integrity. Sure, you can do all the right things, but are you doing them for the right reasons? Or, are you only doing them when you're in front of others to show off your "religion?" Let's bring this home to foster care and adoption, the world in which we all sit. We can look like a perfect

> **"Sure, you can do all the right things, but are you doing them for the right reasons or, are you doing them when you're in front of others to show off your "religion.""**

family on the outside, in church, or in public, but be the complete opposite when we're behind the closed doors of our home, away from public eyes. In public, we control ourselves and put on appearances, but in private, we can be totally ourselves.

So why does James use the tongue as his example? Because of all the members of our body, the tongue is the most likely to betray our true selves. Words matter. How we speak to others, about others, and around others matters. We use our tongue to bless, to curse, to encourage, to tear down, to defend, to accuse, to share truth, and to mutter lies. It is the tongue that exposes us for who we really are, underneath the veneer. Words carry weight, and by them, men have lived or died, marriages have thrived or fallen apart, families have remained close or become strangers, countries have risen or fallen, and wars are fought and won. A person who can control his tongue and submit it to both the authority of the Word and the grace of Jesus, is a person with self-control. A person who cannot bridle his tongue, yet thinks himself religious, is fooling himself, and James declares his religion useless.

We can bring a child into our families through foster care and adoption for all the right reasons. It can look great to do it. All of our neighbors can consider us saints. Our church can put us in the end-of-the-year video highlights. But if behind the curtain, we are stubborn, selfish, critical, and harsh, our efforts are useless, because they will end up ripping apart the very fabric of the family God has called us to create for His glory.

I hope you hear me and understand that I'm not saying you have to go around announcing to the world how terrible things are at home, if that's your story. The point that James is making here is that a wholeheartedly committed believer, whose life is truly centered in Christ wouldn't put on appearances, even in tough times. A fully-committed disciple understands joy in trial.

The gift that James is giving us in this scripture is a warning to closely examine our motives and ask ourselves if our actions are for outward display. Or, are our motives genuine and proven in our actions, moving us forward in obedience to the Lord, no matter the cost.

Scripture Meditation: Take a few moments to read the following Scriptures. Allow the Holy Spirit to speak to your heart about each of them.

> **1 Peter 3:10** "For whoever would love life and see good days must keep their tongue from evil and their lips from deceitful speech."

> **Ephesians 4:29** "Do not let any unwholesome talk come out of your mouths, but only what is helpful for building others up according to their needs, that it may benefit those who listen."

> **Matthew 15:11** "What goes into someone's mouth does not defile them, but what comes out of their mouth, that is what defiles them."

> **Proverbs 21:23** "Those who guard their mouths and their tongues keep themselves from calamity."

Capturing Thoughts: Throughout your adoption journey, I encourage you to capture your thoughts, fears, moments of joy, memories, and challenges. It will be a great encouragement to go back and read what you've written before. Looking back, you'll be surprised how much you and your family grow through your experiences.

Prayer Starter: Jesus, forgive us where we have put on the appearance of righteousness but were faking it. Help us to stand uprightly before you, the same in private as we are in public.

Discussion Questions – Day 29: Useless Religion

1. As an adoptive or foster family, do you often feel the pressure to act like you have it all together? Share this feeling. Are there safe ways you can get the truth out?

2. In today's devotion, Pam says, "We can bring a child into our families

through foster care and adoption for all the right reasons. It can look great to do it. All of our neighbors can consider us saints. Our church can put us in the end of the year video highlights. But if behind the curtain we are stubborn, selfish, critical, and harsh, our efforts are useless, because they will end up ripping apart the very fabric of the family God has called us to create for His glory." Do you struggle with this idea? Talk about what might be challenging you about these words.

3. Is self-control something that you struggle with, regarding your tongue or any other action? Talk about strategies you can implement to reign in these aspects of your life.

4. Is there something that this group can pray for you about this week?

My Journey:

(Use this space to capture your thoughts, prayers, concerns and questions)

PURE AND UNDEFILED RELIGION BEFORE GOD AND THE FATHER IS THIS: TO VISIT ORPHANS IN THEIR TROUBLE, AND TO KEEP ONESELF UNSPOTTED FROM THE WORLD.

JAMES 1:27

DAY 30: PURE & UNDEFILED RELIGION

I'm literally tearing up as I begin to write this last day's devotion. I feel like James Chapter 1 has been a constant companion over the last three years, as God has purified my heart, and I've obediently admonished and encouraged families through its words after every single workshop. Finishing this devotional for publication is like exposing a private conversation that I've been having with my most trusted friend for the past three years. It feels intimate and vulnerable. I'm truthfully undone in all the best ways. God is so good.

James 1:27 is the premier verse in foster care and adoption. You'll find it nearly everywhere you look in places where ministries are promoting the call to become a foster or adoptive parent, and, for good reason—it's perfect. The problem is that it's the last verse in the chapter and therefore, it's the end of the story. As we've learned in the past month, it's far from the fullness of the story we're stepping into when we are obeying the call to bring a child into our lives through foster care or adoption.

Yesterday, we focused on religion as what we do, our actions as believers. Today, we focus on religion as who we are, our very identity. Pure and undefiled religion before God, our Father, is this: ministry to the orphan and widow. It's an echo of Jesus's words "love your neighbor as yourself," to go into someone else's world, their mess, their trouble, their sorrow, their distress, and to love them as much as you love yourself. This "religion" sits with someone who is helpless, alone, and vulnerable, regardless of her circumstance or behavior. It exudes from our pores, because it's just who we are as followers of Christ: people who don't mind getting their hands and feet dirty, walking into a messed up situation, and reaching out to help.

Our children from hard places come to us with a myriad of stuff from their past. This stuff comes out of them in their behaviors, words, and actions. It's right here, right into the center of it all, where God calls us. And as we sit with them in their trouble, totally at a loss as to what to do, and absolutely dependent on Him, He looks down upon us and sees His reflection. A pure reflection of Him in the moment of our weakness and sorrow, on behalf of a vulnerable child looks like our agenda and expectations fading away, into prayer totally devoid of selfish ambition, seeking the will and wisdom of the Father, because there's nothing for us to gain but to see Him glorified.

> **"Our children from hard places come to us with a myriad of stuff from their past. This stuff comes out of them in their behaviors, words, and actions. It's right here, right into the center of it all, that God calls us."**

In the form of His Son, Jesus, God rolled up his sleeves and got His hands dirty walking alongside us in this world. Then with great sorrow and suffering, He gave Himself completely to the Cross in the most profound expression of love this world has ever known. He did this because He was moved with compassion and tenderness for our circumstances, which warranted our death. Touched by the lost nature of our souls, the brokenness of our condition, and the hardness of our hearts, He responded with love and mercy. He poured himself out on our behalf at the cost of his own comfort, even his own human desire. In grace, he dealt with our sins; in mercy, he stepped into our misery. Yet we nailed Him to a Cross and demanded a murderer be set free in His place. It was Jesus who recited the parable of The Good Samaritan. It was He who could never pass by a hurting soul without being moved by compassion to offer the gift of healing. It is this Savior, this Sacrificial Lamb, to whom we pray, "Make me more like you, Jesus." God is answering your prayer. This is our example, the image we are being refined into.

In a sermon on this theme, B.B. Warfield answers the objection people raise to giving money and energy towards a Christian ministry of mercy to orphans and widows; "Objection 1: My money is my own. Answer: Christ might have said, 'My blood is my own, my life is my own'... then where should we have been? Objection 2: The poor are undeserving. Answer: Christ might have said, 'They are wicked rebels... shall I lay my life down for these? I will give to the good angels.' But no, he left the ninety-nine, and came for the lost; he gave his blood for the undeserving. Objection 3: The poor may abuse it. Answer: Christ might have said the same, with far greater truth. Christ knew that thousands would trample his blood under their feet, that most would despise it, that many would make it an excuse for sinning more, yet he gave his own blood. Oh, my dear Christians! If you would be like Christ, give much, give often, give freely, to the vile and poor, the thankless, and the undeserving. Christ is glorious and happy, and so will you be. It is not your money I want, but your happiness. Remember his own word, 'It is more blessed to give than receive.'" (*The Person and Work of Christ,* p.574).

Over the past 30 days, we've taken a journey of biblical order in learning to control ourselves in our thoughts, actions, and reactions. This, in turn, makes us fit to follow Christ into the world and change it by reaching the lost, hurting, and vulnerable, because there simply isn't a choice; it's who we are—from the inside out—because that's who our Savior is, and we look just like Him. It's a gift.

Scripture Meditation: Take a few moments to read the following Scriptures. Allow the Holy Spirit to speak to your heart about each of them.

Psalm 68:5&6 "A father to the fatherless, a defender of widows is God in his holy dwelling. God sets the lonely in families, he leads out the prisoners with singing; but the rebellious live in a sun-scorched land."

Matthew 6:1-4 "Be careful not to practice your righteousness in front of others to be seen by them. If you do, you will have no reward from your Father in heaven. So when you give to the needy, do not announce it with the trumpets, as the hypocrites do in the synagogues and on the streets, to be honored by others. Truly I tell you, they have received their reward in full. But when you give to the needy, do not let your left hand know what your right hand is doing, so that your giving may be in secret. Then your Father, who sees what is done is secret, will reward you openly."

Psalm 82:3 "Defend the weak and the fatherless; uphold the cause of the poor and the oppressed."

Acts 20:35 "In everything I did, I showed you that by this kind of hard work we must help the weak, remembering the words of the Lord Jesus himself said, 'It is more blessed to give than to receive.'"

Capturing Thoughts: Throughout your adoption journey, I encourage you to capture your thoughts, fears, moments of joy, memories, and challenges. It will be a great encouragement to go back and read what you've written before. Looking back, you'll be surprised how much you and your family grow through your experiences.

Prayer Starter: Lord, thank you for this call to minister to our children, even in their distress and trouble. Give us your heart of compassion and mercy, as we seek to guide and love them. Help us to be your hands and feet, a fit and perfect reflection of you.

Discussion Questions – Day 30: Pure & Undefiled Religion

1. Do you find it hard to remember why you're doing this when your children are being especially difficult? Is there a visual reminder that you can set before you where you can see it on a regular basis?

2. In what ways has this study changed your view of God's call to care for your children? Share these with the group.

3. Pam closes this devotional study with this statement, "Over the past 30 days, we've taken a journey of biblical order in learning to control ourselves in our thoughts, actions, and reactions. This, in turn, makes us fit to follow Christ into the world and change it by reaching the lost, hurting, and vulnerable, because there simply isn't a choice; it's who we are—from the inside out—because that's who our Savior is, and we look just like Him. It's a gift." What are some ways that you can remember to celebrate the gift

that God has given you in your family?

4. Listen to the song, "I Won't Give Up" by Jason Mraz. Allow God to minister to your heart and seal a commitment to finish your race in you.

My Journey:

(Use this space to capture your thoughts, prayers, concerns and questions)

ABOUT THE AUTHOR

Pam Parish is the president and founder of Connections Homes, an Atlanta-based nonprofit organization focused on providing family-based home environments where adolescents with difficult pasts and uncertain futures can connect, grow, and belong. She and her husband, Steve, were high school sweethearts. More than two decades later, they are still best friends. At the time of this writing, they have eight daughters and three sons-in-law: Candie Kane, Katya Grace, Tae & Kelsey Joy, Elizabeth Yeaune Harang (Jesus's blessing and love), Tyree & Seara Serenity, Charlie Selah, Paul & Kristan Faith, and Heather Hope. They also have three grandsons, Juan, Jayden and Junior, and one granddaughter, Adrianna. Pam is a foster care and adoption advocate, public speaker, trainer, and family crisis mentor.

Ready or Not for Families Growing Through Foster Care & Adoption

Entering the journey of foster care and adoption can be one of the most daunting decisions that you make as a parent. Parenting a child who has experienced trauma and loss is a rewarding experience, but it's not easy.

In this biblically-centered and straight-forward book, Pam Parish helps parents to:

- Consider the impact of foster care and adoption on their lives and families.
- Evaluate their motives and expectations for the foster care and adoption experience.
- Explore foster care and adoption through the lens of scripture.

A Scripture-based Guide for Parenting in the Trenches

From the moment a child enters our life, parenting is a tough job. It's even harder when a child is struggling with difficult behaviors—defiance, rejection, running away, drug addiction, sexual misconduct, criminal activity, attachment issues, rage, and more. Parenting in crisis leaves parents worn out from exhaustion, frustration, and fear.

God doesn't leave us, even in the midst of our fears, failures, and fatigue. In this powerful second devotional for foster and adoptive families, Pam encourages and challenges the *Battle-Weary Parent*.

Connect With Pam Online

 @pamparish

 facebook.com/pamparish

 pinterest.com/pamparish

 google.com/+pamparish

Pam also shares inspiration for foster and adoptive parents on her blog: **pamparish.com**.

To inquire about having Pam speak at your church, agency or conference visit pamparish.com/contact.

Scripture has much to say about about orphans. Here's a list of verses that mention the fatherless and orphan.

Exodus 22:22-24

Do not take advantage of a widow or an **orphan**. If you do and they cry out to me, I will certainly hear their cry. My anger will be aroused, and I will kill you with the sword; your wives will become widows and your children **fatherless**.

Deuteronomy 10:18

He defends the cause of the **fatherless** and the widow, and loves the alien, giving him food and clothing.

Deuteronomy 14:29

So that the Levites (who have no allotment or inheritance of their own) and the aliens, the **fatherless** and the widows who live in your towns may come and eat and be satisfied, and so that the LORD your God may bless you in all the work of your hands.

Deuteronomy 16:11

And rejoice before the LORD your God at the place he will choose as a dwelling for his Name—you, your sons and daughters, your menservants and maidservants, the Levites in your towns, and the aliens, the **fatherless** and the widows living among you.

Deuteronomy 16:14

Be joyful at your Feast--you, your sons and daughters, your menservants and maidservants, and the Levites, the aliens, the **fatherless** and the widows who live in your towns.

Deuteronomy 24:17

Do not deprive the alien or the **fatherless** of justice, or take the cloak of the widow as a pledge.

Deuteronomy 24:19-21

When you are harvesting in your field and you overlook a sheaf, do not go back to get it. Leave it for the alien, the **fatherless** and the widow, so that the LORD your God may bless you in all the work of your hands. When you beat the olives from your trees, do not go over the branches a second time. Leave what remains for the alien, the **fatherless** and the widow. When you harvest the grapes in your vineyard, do not go over the vines again. Leave what remains for the alien, the **fatherless** and the widow.

Deuteronomy 26:12 -13

When you have finished setting aside a tenth of all your produce in the third year, the year of the tithe, you shall give it to the Levite, the alien, the **fatherless** and the widow, so that they may eat in your towns and be satisfied. Then say to the LORD your God: "I have removed from my house the sacred portion and have given it to the Levite, the alien, the **fatherless** and the widow, according to all you commanded. I have not turned aside from your commands nor have I forgotten any of them.

Deuteronomy 27:19

"Cursed is the man who withholds justice from the alien, the **fatherless** or the widow." Then all the people shall say, "Amen!"

Job 6:27

You would even cast lots for the **fatherless** and barter away your friend.

Job 22:7-11

You gave no water to the weary and you withheld food from the hungry, though you were a powerful man, owning land-- an honored man, living on it. And you sent widows away empty-handed and broke the strength of the **fatherless**. That is why snares are all around you, why sudden peril terrifies you, why it is so dark you cannot see, and why a flood of water covers you.

Job 24:2-4

Men move boundary stones; they pasture flocks they have stolen. They drive away the **orphan's** donkey and take the widow's ox in pledge. They thrust the needy from the path and force all the poor of the land into hiding.

Job 24:9

The **fatherless** child is snatched from the breast; the infant of the poor is seized for a debt.

Job 29:11-12

Whoever heard me spoke well of me, and those who saw me commended me, because I rescued the poor who cried for help, and the **fatherless** who had none to assist him.

Job 31:16-18

"If I have denied the desires of the poor or let the eyes of the widow grow weary, if I have kept my bread to myself, not sharing it with the **fatherless** - but from my youth I reared him as would a father, and from my birth I guided the widow.

Job 31:21-22

If I have raised my hand against the **fatherless**, knowing that I had influence in court, then let my arm fall from the shoulder, let it be broken off at the joint.

Psalm 10:14

But you, O God, do see trouble and grief; you consider it to take it in hand. The victim commits himself to you; you are the helper of the **fatherless**.

Psalm 10:17-18

You hear, O LORD, the desire of the afflicted; you encourage them, and you listen to their cry, defending the **fatherless** and the oppressed, in order that man, who is of the earth, may terrify no more.

Psalm 68:5-6

A father to the **fatherless**, a defender of widows, is God in his holy dwelling. God sets the lonely in families, he leads forth the prisoners with singing; but the rebellious live in a sun-scorched land.

Psalm 82:3-4

Defend the cause of the weak and **fatherless**; maintain the rights of the poor and oppressed. Rescue the weak and needy; deliver them from the hand of the wicked.

Psalm 94:6

They slay the widow and the alien; they murder the **fatherless**.

Psalm 146:9

The LORD watches over the alien and sustains the **fatherless** and the widow, but he frustrates the ways of the wicked.

Proverbs 23:10-11

Do not move an ancient boundary stone or encroach on the fields of the **fatherless**, for their Defender is strong; he will take up their case against you.

Isaiah 1:17

Learn to do right! Seek justice, encourage the oppressed. Defend the cause of the **fatherless**, plead the case of the widow.

Isaiah 1:23

Our rulers are rebels, companions of thieves; they all love bribes and chase after gifts. They do not defend the cause of the **fatherless**; the widow's case does not come before them.

Isaiah 9:17

Therefore the Lord will take no pleasure in the young men, nor will he pity the **fatherless** and widows, for everyone is ungodly and wicked, every mouth speaks vileness. Yet for all this, his anger is not turned away, his hand is still upraised.

Isaiah 10:1-2

Woe to those who make unjust laws, to those who issue oppressive decrees, to deprive the poor of their rights and withhold justice from the oppressed of my people, making widows their prey and robbing the **fatherless**.

Jeremiah 5:27-29

Like cages full of birds, their houses are full of deceit; they have become rich and powerful and have grown fat and sleek. Their evil deeds have no limit; they do not plead the case of the **fatherless** to win it, they do not defend the rights of the poor. Should I not punish them for this?" declares the LORD. "Should I not avenge myself on such a nation as this?"

Jeremiah 7:5-7

If you really change your ways and your actions and deal with each other justly, if you do not oppress the alien, the **fatherless** or the widow and do not shed innocent blood in this place, and if you do not follow other gods to your own harm, then I will let you live in this place, in the land I gave your forefathers for ever and ever.

Jeremiah 22:3

This is what the LORD says: Do what is just and right. Rescue from the hand of his oppressor the one who has been robbed. Do no wrong or violence to the alien, the **fatherless** or the widow, and do not shed innocent blood in this place.

Jeremiah 49:11

Leave your **orphans**; I will protect their lives. Your widows too can trust in me.

Ezekiel 22:7

In you they have treated father and mother with contempt; in you they have oppressed the alien and mistreated the **fatherless** and the widow.

Hosea 14:3

Assyria cannot save us; we will not mount war-horses. We will never again say 'Our gods' to what our own hands have made, for in you the **fatherless** find compassion.

Zechariah 7:10

Do not oppress the widow or the **fatherless**, the alien or the poor. In your hearts do not think evil of each other.

Malachi 3:5

So I will come near to you for judgment. I will be quick to testify against sorcerers, adulterers and perjurers, against those who defraud laborers of their wages, who oppress the widows and the **fatherless**, and deprive aliens of justice, but do not fear me," says the LORD Almighty.

John 14:18

I will not leave you as **orphans**; I will come to you.

James 1:27

Religion that God our Father accepts as pure and faultless is this: to look after **orphans** and widows in their distress and to keep oneself from being polluted by the world.